THE FIRST PERSON

An Essay on Reference and Intentionality

THE FIRST PERSON

*An Essay on Reference
and Intentionality*

by RODERICK M. CHISHOLM

UNIVERSITY OF MINNESOTA PRESS
MINNEAPOLIS

Roderick M. Chisholm is Andrew W. Mellon Professor of Humanities in the Department of Philosophy at Brown University. He is a past president of the American Philosophical Association and author of many articles and books (including *Perceiving: A Philosophical Study*, *Person and Object: A Metaphysical Study*, and *Theory of Knowledge*).

Copyright © 1981 by The Royal Institute of Philosophy
All rights reserved.
Published by the University of Minnesota Press,
2037 University Avenue Southeast,
Minneapolis MN 55414

Printed in Great Britain

Library of Congress Cataloging in Publication Data
Chisholm, Roderick M
  The first person, an essay on reference
and intentionality
  Includes bibliographical references and index.
  1. Reference (Philosophy) 2. Intention (Logic)
I. Title.
B105.R25C44   160   80-24910
ISBN 0-8166-1045-2
     0-8166-1075-4 (pbk)

The University of Minnesota
is an equal-opportunity
educator and employer.

CONTENTS

Acknowledgements vii

1 Introduction 1
2 The Ontological Background 4
3 The Problem of First Person Sentences 13
4 Indirect Attribution 27
5 The Interpretation of Demonstratives 41
6 On the Meaning of Proper Names 54
7 Certainty and the Unity of Consciousness 75
8 Transcendent Evidence and Perception 92
9 Knowledge and Belief *De Re* 107

Appendix The Ontology of States of Affairs 123
Index 133

ACKNOWLEDGEMENTS

I wish to express my special indebtedness to the following people: to H. D. Lewis and Godfrey Vesey who were, respectively, the Chairman of the Council and the Executive Secretary of the Royal Institute of Philosophy when these lectures were presented before the Institute in May 1979; to Rudolf Haller and Ernest Sosa for the issue of the *Grazer Philosophische Studien* (Vol. VII, 1979) which enabled me to refine upon and correct the philosophical views that led to the present book; to the contributors to that issue; to Asa Kasher and the contributors to the July 1978 issue of *Philosophia: Philosophical Quarterly of Israel*; and to Elizabeth Anscombe, who consented to my use of 'The First Person', a title she had given to her Wolfson College Lecture in 1974. I wish also to acknowledge my indebtedness to Herbert Heidelberger and Ernest Sosa, who have read and criticized parts of this work, and to the students and colleagues with whom I have discussed these questions. I mention, finally, my association with George Katkov and Rudolf Haller, which has been invaluable in helping me to retain what I believe is a sound philosophical perspective.

I also thank the editors and publishers of the following books and journals for giving me permission to adapt parts of the following published papers for the present book: 'Objects and Persons', *Grazer Philosophische Studien*, VII (1979); 'The Indirect Reflexive', in C. Diamond and J. Teichman, eds., *Intention and Intentionality* (Harvester: 1979); 'The Logic of Believing', *Pacific Philosophical Quarterly*, 61 (1980); 'A Version of Foundationalism', *Midwest Studies in Philosophy*, V (1980); and 'The Meaning of Proper Names', *Proceedings of the Fourth International Wittgenstein Symposium, 1979* (Vienna: Holder, Pichler, Tempsky, 1980).

Chapter 1
INTRODUCTION

IN this book I attempt to deal philosphically with the ancient question: How is objective reference—or intentionality—possible? How is it possible for one thing to direct its thoughts upon another thing? Wittgenstein summarized the question by asking: 'What makes my idea of him an idea of *him*?'[1]

Many would answer Wittgenstein's question in this way: 'My idea is an idea of *him* because I have a *language* in which there are terms that refer to him and I use one of those terms in my inner speech to myself'. But the question also has its analogue for terms or names and hence for language: 'What makes a word that refers to him a word that refers to *him*?' And the traditional answer to *that* question takes us back to our original question: 'The word is associated with a thought that refers to him—it expresses an *idea* of him'.

Thus we may distinguish two different approaches to our problem. Are we to explicate the facts of reference and intentionality in terms of certain facts about language, or are we to explicate these facts about language in terms of intentionality? If we take the first approach, we may be said to presuppose the primacy of the intentional. If we take the second, we may be said to presuppose the primacy of the linguistic.

I shall here take the first approach.

I shall propose that the primary form of all reference is that reference to ourselves that we normally express when we use the first-person pronoun. In the case of believing, this reference may be called 'direct attribution'. Our reference to all other things is *by way of* such reference to ourselves. I shall argue that, although we express ourselves in first-person *sentences*, the reference to ourselves that we thus express does *not* involve the acceptance of first-person *propositions*—for, I shall contend, there is no good reason to assume that there *are* such propositions. The primary form of believing is not a matter of accepting propositions; it is a matter of attributing *properties* to oneself. I am the primary *object* of my own attributions and the properties are the *content*.

The great majority of philosophers and linguists who have concerned themselves with reference and with the meanings of sentences have assumed that indicative sentences containing first-person pronouns—as well as those containing other demonstratives and proper names—are used primarily to express propositions.[2] And this assumption has led to an ontology which is often left implicit and is seldom defended.

I shall begin by setting forth certain ontological theses which this book presupposes. I shall say that these theses serve to 'purify' our ontology, since they enable us to dispense with the superfluous non-Platonic entities in which most contemporary theories of reference and intentionality are entangled. This book may be thought of as being, in part, a defence of the purified ontology.

I shall then turn to 'the problem of first-person sentences'. I shall attempt to show that the most plausible solution to that problem is one that construes the person himself as being the primary object of all his intentional attitudes. I shall consider the use of the first-person pronoun and explicate that use by reference to the distinction between object and content referred to above. This explication of the first-person pronoun, I shall suggest, gives us the key to the proper understanding of the uses of other demonstratives and proper names. We shall then be in a position to explicate linguistic reference in terms of the facts of intentionality.

The three final chapters have to do with *justified* objective reference. Hence we shall be concerned with epistemology or theory of knowledge—a topic which, I believe, has been somewhat neglected outside the United States. I shall consider the nature of empirical certainty—something which has only the first person as its object—and then discuss the 'unity of consciousness' and the sense in which each person may be said to be 'directly acquainted' with himself. Then I shall consider the relation between the directly evident facts about ourselves and the rest of what we know. And, finally, given a theory of knowledge, we will be able to complete our answer to the question of Wittgenstein with which we have begun.

Notes

1 *Philosophical Investigations* (Oxford: Basil Blackwell, 1953), p. 177. The official English translation here uses 'image' instead of 'idea'. The German is: 'Was macht meine Vorstellung von ihm zu einer Vorstellung zu *ihm*?''
2 Exceptions are David Lewis and John Perry. Compare Lewis's 'Attitudes De Dictor and De Se', *Philosophical Review*, LXXXVIII (1979), pp. 513–43, and the following papers by Perry: 'Frege on Demonstratives', *Philosophical Review*, LXXXVI (1977), pp. 474–97, and 'The Problem of the Essential Indexical', *Nous*, XIII (1979), pp. 3–21.

Chapter 2
THE ONTOLOGICAL BACKGROUND

Introduction

THE theory of reference and intention is, in part, an ontology—a theory about what there is, in the strict and philosophical sense of the expression 'there is'. In the present chapter, I shall sketch the ontology that is presupposed by the theory of reference and intentionality to be set forth in the present book. The reader who is interested in intentionality and reference but not in ontology may profitably omit this chapter, but such a reader will now know why it is I have resisted the easy moves that are typical of most contemporary theories of reference.

What there is includes, of course, individual things and parts of individual things. Possibly it includes, in addition, heaps or aggregates of individual things and of parts of individual things. And possibly it also includes the boundaries of certain individual things—i.e. points, lines and surfaces. But what of those entities that are *not* individual things—and are not parts or aggregates or boundaries of individual things?

The ontology that I shall develop here is Platonistic, since it presupposes that there are *eternal*, or *abstract*, objects. It presupposes, in other words, that in the strict and philosophical sense of the expression 'there are', there *are* properties, relations and states of affairs. In this respect, I believe, the present theory is not unlike that presupposed by most other contemporary theories of reference. But the present theory is 'purified' in that it refuses to countenance certain *non*-Platonic entities which are prominent in almost all the other theories. These non-Platonic entities may be suggested by the following expressions: *indexical properties* ('the property of being identical with that thing'); *singular propositions* (the propositions said to be expressed by such sentences as 'I am sitting' and 'That man is standing'); *times*, considered as particular things which may be designated by dates and by other temporal expressions; and *possible worlds*, considered as particular things and many of them such that they contain the individuals of the actual world.

THE ONTOLOGICAL BACKGROUND 5

The present book is intended to show, in part, that such non-Platonic entities are superfluous.

In this chapter, I shall set forth the positive theory of properties and states of affairs that is here presupposed. In the *Appendix*, I shall consider states of affairs in more detail, noting the sense in which they may be said to have a *structure*, and showing how *propositions*, *times* and *possible worlds* may be construed as sub-species of states of affairs.

The undefined philosophical locutions that we will make use of in the present chapter are these: (i) '*x* exemplifies *y*'; (ii) '*x* is possibly such that it is *F*'; (iii) '*x* conceives *y*'; (iv) '*x* obtains'; and (v) '*x* is a relation'. It would be difficult, if not impossible, to formulate an adequate ontology without making use of similar locutions.

A Purified Theory of Properties

I assume that any adequate theory of properties or attributes will presuppose that there *are* properties or attributes and that some but not all of them are exemplified. There is the property of *being a dog*, which is exemplified, and there is also the property of *being a unicorn*, which is not exemplified. The assumption that there are *unexemplified* as well as exemplified properties is sometimes taken as a mark of 'extreme realism'. How, then, can we call the present theory a 'purified' theory?

In countenancing the existence of properties that correspond to some predicative expressions ('round', 'square', 'unicorn'), we do not thereby countenance properties corresponding to *every* predicative expression. We know, after all, that 'The word "French" is inapplicable to itself' should not be taken to say that the word 'French' has the *property* of being inapplicable to itself; for we are led to contradictions if we assumed that there *is* such a property. ('Does the property of being inapplicable to itself have the property of being inapplicable to itself?') What we are told by the sentence: 'The word "French" is inapplicable to itself', is that the word 'French' does *not* have the property of being applicable to itself.

Wittgenstein once observed that a fundamental philosophical error is that of supposing that there is a substance answering to every substantive. We may add that another fundamental philosophical error is that of supposing that there is a property corresponding to every predicate. I shall assume, then, that certain types of predicative expression need not be construed as having properties as their senses. One consequence of the assumption is that certain types of well-formed, meaningful, indicative sentences need not be construed as expressing propositions or states of affairs.

Let us *define* the concept of a property as follows:

D1 x is a property = Df x is possibly such that there is something that exemplifies it.

Our definition makes use of two undefined concepts, that of exemplification ('x exemplifies y') and that of *de re* possibility ('x is possibly such that it is F').

There may seem to be an obvious objection to our definition. One may say: 'But the property of being both round and square is not possibly such that there is something that exemplifies it!' The reply is this: There is the property of being round and the property of being square; there is also the property of being non-round and the property of being non-square; but there is no reason for supposing that there is the property of being both round and square.[1]

Ostensible commitment to unexemplifiable properties is easily explained away. Thus 'Nothing has the property of being both round and square' becomes 'Nothing has both the property of being round and the property of being square'. What of 'Nothing is such that, for every x, it shaves x, if, and only if, x does not shave x'? This would become: 'Nothing has both (a) the property of being such that, for every x, it shaves x if x does not shave x, and also (b) the property of being such that, for every x, it shaves x if x does not shave x'.

I shall assume that what we say about properties may also be said, *mutatis mutandis*, about relations. I shall assume, in particular, that for every relation, there is a set of properties which is necessarily such that those properties are exemplified if and only if there are things that stand in that relation. The concept expressed by 'standing in' is obviously analogous to the concept expressed by 'exemplifying'. But, since I do not here develop a theory of relations, we include '*relation*' among our undefined terms.

Conceivability

The concept of a property is inseparably connected with the concept of *conceiving*. Indeed, I believe, we may affirm the following general principle:

P1 Every property is possibly such that there is someone who conceives it.

Conceiving is the third undefined concept of our ontology.

A corollary of the above principle is the fact that every property—except those properties entailed by the property of conceiving—is necessarily such that it can be conceived even if it is not exemplified. (A property P may be said to *entail* a property Q, provided only that P is necessarily such that, if it is exemplified, then Q is exemplified, and whoever conceives it conceives Q.) Hence we may say:

P2 Consider any property (other than the property of conceiving and what it entails): if the property is possibly such that nothing exemplifies it, then it is possibly such that (a) nothing exemplifies it and (b) something conceives it.

This principle implies that no property is such that it can be conceived only by reference to a contingent thing. If this is true, as it seems to be to be, then we can say of properties something very much like what Spinoza said of substance: a property is that which 'is in itself and is conceived through itself; in other words, it is that the conception of which does not need the conception of any other thing from which it must be formed'.[2] But, since some properties are compounds of other properties and therefore cannot be conceived unless their components are conceived, we should modify our Spinozistic statement so as to say: 'A property is that which is conceived either through itself or through another property; it is that the conception of which does not require the conception of anything that might not have existed'. I take this to imply that, although some properties can be conceived only by reference to other properties, no property is such that it can be conceived only by reference to some individual thing.

Hence it is problematic whether terms and predicates containing demonstratives (for example, 'the owner of *this* book' and 'sitting next to *that* man') will have properties as their senses. We shall not presuppose that there are such 'indexical' or 'referential' properties. In the following chapter, we shall consider in detail the reasons there are for saying that the demonstrative pronoun 'I' has a property as its sense. We shall see that these reasons are hardly adequate, and we shall subsequently find a more plausible way of interpreting this pronoun. We shall then be in a position to interpret the meaning of other demonstrative expressions—which we shall do in Chapters 5 and 6.

Given the principle we have just set forth, it would also seem to be problematic whether monadic predicate expressions containing free variables have properties as their senses. If this is true, then, although we may affirm: 'Necessarily, for every x, x is identical with x', we should not affirm: 'For every x, x necessarily has the property of being identical with x'. For there will be no property corresponding to the expression 'the property of being identical with x.' (To say this is not to reject the *relation* of identity. There *is* a relation of identity, and each thing bears the relation of identity to itself.)

How are we to decide whether a predicative expression has a property as its sense? We could ask what is sense *would* be if it *had* a sense. Then, if we find that the supposed sense would not conform to the principles here set forth, we shall look for another way of interpreting the expression. And if we find one, then our 'purified' conception of properties will be to that extent confirmed.

We shall also adopt the following maxim. If a predicate expression contains, as one of its parts, a predicative expression which need not be construed as having a property as its sense, then the longer expression need not be construed as having a property as its sense. For example, if 'being taller than that man' does not thus correspond to a property, then 'being wise and taller than that man' does not correspond to a property.

We shall not assume that, in *addition* to properties, there are such entities as classes or sets. But we shall occasionally speak of classes, keeping in mind that statements ostensibly about classes can be reduced to statements about properties. Thus, following Russell once again, we can interpret 'The class of things that are F is G' as telling us this: For every property H, if H is exemplified by all and only those things that exemplify the property of being F, then H has the property of being G.[3]

We may be said to *conceive* a class, or a set, to the extent that we conceive one of the properties that is common and peculiar to its members.

Numbers, too, may be thought of as properties—more specifically, as properties of properties. Thus the number five is the property of having five instances—a property which is exemplified by any property which is exemplified by five things.

States of Affairs

By making use of the concept of *obtaining* (occurring, taking place), we may now characterize states of affairs.

There is a close connection between the concept of obtaining and that of a state of affairs, but we should not express this concept by saying that a state of affairs is something which is possibly such that it obtains. For some states of affairs—for example, there being round squares—are not possibly such that they obtain. In characterizing states of affairs, we shall appeal rather to this fact: Every state of affairs is necessarily such that whoever conceives it conceives something that possibly obtains. Thus, whoever conceives *there being round squares*, which is *not* possibly such that it obtains, also conceives *there being squares*, which *is* possibly such that it obtains. It will not, however, be enough to define 'state of affairs' by saying merely: 'A state of affairs is that which is necessarily such that whoever conceives it conceives something that obtains', for it is possible that such a formula also holds of *properties*. It may be, for example, that it is not possible to conceive *redness* without conceiving *something being red*. Hence we should add to the definition a clause saying that a state of affairs is not a property or a relation.

Our definition is therefore:

D2 *p* is a state of affairs = Df *p* is necessarily such that (i) it is possible that there is someone who conceives it, (ii) whoever conceives it conceives something which is possibly such that it obtains and (iii) it is not a property or a relation.

Sometimes states of affairs that do not obtain are described as 'merely possible entities'. But surely, no one who takes ontology seriously would maintain that there *are* certain things that are merely possible and not actual. States of affairs—whether or not they obtain and whether or not they are self-consistent—are not 'merely possible entities'; like everything else, they exist. (We shall discuss 'possible worlds' in the *Appendix* to this book.)

'If all states of affairs exist, what does it mean to say that some are merely possible and that others are impossible?' To say of a state of affairs that it is 'merely possible' is to say of it (i) that it does not obtain and (ii) that it is possibly such that it does obtain. And analogously for the other modal predicates that are applied to states of affairs.

The Relations between States of Affairs and Properties

States of affairs, like the sentences that express them, may be subdivided into those that are 'compound' and those that are 'non-compound', and 'non-compound' states of affairs may be subdivided, in turn, into those that are affirmative and those that are negative. (The nature of and justification for these distinctions will be discussed in the *Appendix* to this book.)

Non-compound states of affairs are related to properties in the following respects. Those that are affirmative are such that, for certain properties, the states of affairs obtain if and only if the properties are exemplified. The states of affairs may then be said to *imply* the properties. Similarly, those that are negative are such that, for certain properties, the states of affairs obtain if and only if the properties are not exemplified. The states of affairs may then be said to *exclude* the properties.

What we have said may be put as a general principle about states of affairs and their relation to properties.

P4　For every non-compound state of affairs p, either (i) there is a non-empty set A of properties such that p obtains if and only if all the members of A are exemplified, or (ii) there is a non-empty set N of properties such that P obtains if and only if none of the members of N is exemplified.

States of affairs, then, are 'pure' or 'qualitative' in very much the same sense as that in which we have said that properties are pure or qualitative. If there is no property corresponding to the indexical expression 'sitting next to that man', then there is no state of affairs or proposition corresponding to the sentence 'Someone is sitting next to that man'. Hence the existence of first-person propositions—and, more generally, the existence of so-called singular propositions—becomes problematic.[4]

We shall not assume that, in addition to states of affairs, there are also such things as 'concrete events', or 'events as particulars'. We shall assume, instead, that all discourse that is ostensibly about events may be reduced to discourse about states of affairs, relations and properties, and individual things.

One may, of course, *define* a category of 'singular propositions', as well as a category of 'concrete events', in terms of states of affairs, relations and properties, and individual things. In saying that the existence of such entities is problematic, I mean to imply only that there is no need to suppose that there are such things *in addition to* the entities countenanced here.

I shall assume, finally, that properties and states of affairs are eternal—or abstract—objects. The vocabulary we have just introduced enables us to say just what an eternal object is. If a thing z is an *eternal object*, then: there is a property H which is such that (a) x has H necessarily and (b) nothing other than x can possibly have H; and there is a state of affairs p which is such that p implies H and p necessarily obtains. In other words, eternal objects have essences (for the *essence* of a thing x is a property which is necessarily such that x exemplifies it and nothing else can possibly exemplify it). And to say that such objects are eternal is to say that there are necessary states of affairs which imply the essences of those objects.

Eternal objects, so defined, are not dependent for their being upon anything which is such that it might not have existed. Also, it follows from what we have said that every eternal object is conceivable—in other words, that every eternal object is possibly such that there is someone who conceives it.

Conclusion

The theory of intentionality and reference that is to be developed here presupposes, then, the ontology that has just been set forth. We shall therefore withhold commitment to any type of entity that does not conform to the ontological categories that have been here introduced.

One may feel that it is impossible to develop an adequate theory of belief and reference without the assumption of the kinds of entities we have held to be superfluous. For the theory of belief and reference is concerned with matters that are most naturally expressed in English by using sentences with impure predicates. Examples are: 'There is someone I am talking with'; 'There is someone sitting next to that man'; 'There is someone sitting next to Tom'; 'He and she both believe that I am taller than you'; and 'John believes, with respect to Karl, that he, Karl, once thought that he, John, was envious of him'.

The interpretation of such statements constitutes the subject-matter of the present book.

Notes

1 But the type of paradox mentioned above makes it clear we should no assume that *every* property has a negation.
2 'By *substance*, I mean that which is in itself, and is conceived through itself; in other words, that of which a conception can be formed independently of any other conception.' *Ethics*, Part I, Definition III.
3 Compare Bertrand Russell, *Logic and Knowledge* (London: Allen & Unwin, Ltd., 1956), p. 89; Rudolf Carnap, *Meaning and Necessity* (Chicago: The University of Chicago Press, 1956), p. 151.
4 Compare A. N. Whitehead and Bertrand Russell: 'Truly elementary judgments are not very easily found'. *Principia Mathematica*, Second Edition, Vol. I (Cambridge: The University Press, 1925), p. 45. Compare also Russell's *Logic and Knowledge*, pp. 201 ff.

Chapter 3

THE PROBLEM OF FIRST-PERSON SENTENCES

Belief *De Re*

WHAT makes my belief about you, then, a belief about *you*?

Let us look for the simplest answer possible. By 'the simplest answer', I mean, not only the answer that is easiest to understand, but also the one that involves the fewest philosophical commitments—the fewest commitments about the nature of the world and the fewest commitments about the faculties and potentialities of the thinking or referring person.

What we are considering is what has come to be known as *de re* belief. A believer may attribute a property to another thing—and do so in such a way that the other thing can be said to be the *object* of his belief, to be *believed about* by him. I may attribute to you, for example, the property of being seated. In this case, we may say that I believe, *with respect to you*, that you are seated. And this means that *you* are such that you are believed by me to be seated. To be believed by someone to be seated may not be much of a property; it is a *denominatio mere extrinsica*. But it *is* something that is true of you and, under some circumstances, it could turn out to be very important.

We are asking, then: What is it for me thus to have a belief with respect to you? How is it that, thus acting at a distance, I make you such that you are believed by me to be seated?

There have been people who have been sceptical about the possibility of this kind of belief *de re*. Some philosophers would say, of you, that you cannot be believed about by me. According to them, it cannot be a property of you—or of any other thing—to be a thing which is such that it is believed by some other thing to be seated. This denial of the possibility of belief *de re*—and of other intentional attitudes *de re*—is obviously a kind of scepticism. it may recall the doctrine philosophers once expressed by saying: 'The mind cannot get outside the circle of its own ideas', and one must deal with it in the way in which one deals with scepticism in general. I would propose that we do not consider *that* question at the present time, for we are assuming that you can be believed about by me and I can be believed about by you.

In my book *Person and Object*, and elsewhere, I had suggested that we could characterize *de re* belief in terms of *de dicto* belief. I had assumed, in other words, that all believing is a matter of accepting some proposition or state of affairs. The theory was essentially this: If I have a belief (*de re*) with respect to you, then I accept (*de dicto*) a proposition or state of affairs which *implies something* with respect to you. The theory presupposed, then, that we be able to say what it is for a proposition or state of affairs to 'imply something with respect to you'. My idea was this: we may say that a proposition *implies* a property provided the proposition is necessarily such that if it is true then something has that property; now some of your properties are identifying properties—they are such that only one thing can have them at a time; and so, if a proposition implies the conjunction of one of your identifying properties with some other property, then the proposition may be said to imply, *with respect to you*, that you have that other property. Hence the proposition 'implies something with respect to you'. This enables us to say that, if I accept (*de dicto*) such a proposition, then I believe, with respect to you, that you have the property in question. The definition I had given was this:

x believes that y has the property of being F = Df y has a property z such that only one thing can have z at a time, and x accepts a proposition implying the conjunction of z and the property of being F.

For example, if you are the tallest man and I accept the proposition that the tallest man is seated, then I accept a proposition which implies the conjunction of one of your identifying properties—that of being the tallest man—with the property of being seated. Hence the theory allows us to say that I believe, with respect to you, that you are seated.

This is a relatively simple theory of *de re* belief. It presupposes that believing is primarily propositional, and it is committed to the being of propositions as well as to the ability of persons to grasp and accept propositions. It also presupposes the being of properties and the ability to conceive both propositions and properties. I am confident that we must make these presuppositions, no matter what our theory of reference may be, but I think that the theory as I have spelled it out presupposes too much. For it has some strange consequences with respect to the nature of propositions and also with respect to the nature of the human mind.

A Difficulty with the Propositional Theory

I suggest that, to see the implausibility of the propositional theory of belief, we consider what the theory involves when it is applied to those beliefs that we have about *ourselves*. If I can be said to believe, with respect to you, that you are sitting, then, surely, I can also be said to believe, with respect to *me*, that I am standing. Given the propositional theory, what would this latter imply?

It would imply that I accept a proposition which implies, with respect to me, that I am standing—hence that I accept a proposition which implies the conjunction of one of my identifying properties with the property of standing.

It may be tempting to say, then, that just as there are first-person sentences—for example, the English sentence 'I am standing'—there are also first-person propositions. The proposition that you accept when, say, you believe yourself to be standing would not be the same as the one I accept when I believe myself to be standing—even though we both use the first-person sentence 'I am standing'. Where my proposition implies one of my identifying properties, yours implies one of yours.

But *what* identifying properties do these propositions imply? If I say, without giving undue thought to myself, 'I am standing', *what* identifying property of me is involved in what I thus believe?

One may be tempted to reason this way: 'If there is an identifying property of me which is implied by the first-person proposition I would express by 'I am standing', then, it would seem, this property can be only the property of *being identical with me*. After all, what *other* property could it be? But if *being identical with me* is a property that I have, then it must be my individual essence or haecceity. For *being identical with me* would be a property that I necessarily have and one that no other thing can possibly have. It would therefore seem reasonable to conclude that I, at least, have an individual essence or haecceity'. Is this reasoning valid?

Some philosophers—for example, Frege and Husserl—have suggested that each of us has his own idea of himself, his own *Ich-Vorstellung* or individual concept. And some of the things that such philosophers have said suggest the following view: The word 'I', in the vocabulary of each person who uses it, has for its referent that person himself and has for its sense that person's *Ich-Vorstellung* or individual concept. The difference between my 'I'-propositions and yours would lie in the fact that mine imply my *Ich-Vorstellung* and not yours, and that yours imply your *Ich-Vorstellung* and not mine.[1]

Could we make a list of *Ich-Vorstellungen*, a list of individual concepts, as we might make a list of colours? We could make a list of colours and then go on to say: 'This first colour is the colour of that thing, this second colour is the colour of that other thing, and this third colour is the colour of that third thing.' But surely we cannot make a list of *Ich-Vorstellungen* in this way and go on to say: 'Here is the *Ich-Vorstellung* that that person expresses in his "I"-sentences, here is the one that that second person expresses in *his* "I"-sentences . . .'

Brentano says that we *never* grasp any properties that are individuating. According to him, any property of mine that I am readily able to grasp is one which, theoretically at least, can be exemplified in several different things at once.[2] Isn't this plausible?

It seems doubtful that I can ever be said thus to grasp thus my own individual essence or haecceity. If I were able to grasp it, shouldn't I also be able to single out its various marks? Perhaps I can single out *some* of the marks of my individual essence—if I have one. Thus it may include various universal essential properties (for example, being red or non-red, or being a musician if a violinist). And perhaps I can single out certain non-universal essential properties (for example, being an individual thing and being a person). But if I can grasp my individual essence, then I ought also to be able to single out in it those features that are unique to it. If *being identical with me* is my individual essence and *being identical with you* is yours, then, presumably, each analyses into personhood and something else as well—one something else in my case and another in yours —but I haven't the faintest idea what this something else might be.

The property, if there is one, which is intended by the expression 'being identical with me' would seem to be extraordinarily empty.

We have these two options, then, so far as individual essences are concerned. First, we could say that, although each of us has an individual essence, these individual essences involve certain properties that are 'unanalysable' and yet *also* such as to be restricted to a single thing. But if *being identical with me* implies personhood, then it is at least *partially* analysable. Hence we would have to say that my individual essence contains an unanalysable part—and it is in that unanalysable part that the difference between my individual essence and yours is to be found.

The second possibility is to say that we have been too readily attracted to the assumption that each individual has an individual essence that he can grasp. This latter course seems to be to be the right one.

One may now be led to say: 'Then my first-person propositions must be interpreted in some other way'. But let us consider an even more far-reaching hypothesis. This is the hypothesis that, although there *are* such things as propositions, which can be expressed in certain types of well-formed sentence, and although there *are* first-person sentences, there are *no* such things as first-person propositions.

Let us also be prepared to accept the more general hypothesis, according to which the normal function of sentences containing demonstrative terms and proper names is *not* that of expressing propositions.

The problem of the 'He, Himself' Locution

We were trying, then, to find a simple account of *de re* belief—of the way in which, for example, I could be said to make you my object and thus have a belief with respect to you. We had a relatively simple account of such belief, but it seemed to break down in application to beliefs about *oneself*—for example, in application to my belief that I am standing. Let us now look at these cases somewhat more carefully, for they involve complications we have not yet considered. These complications pertain to what might be called 'the problem of the "he, himself" locution'.

The 'he, himself' locution may be illustrated by an example that Ernst Mach cites in the second edition of the *Analysis of Sensations*. He writes: 'Not long ago, after a trying railway journey by night, and much fatigued, I got into an omnibus, just as another gentleman appeared at the other end. "What shabby pedagogue is that, that has just entered?" thought I. It was myself; opposite me hung a large mirror. The physiognomy of my class, accordingly, was better known to me than my own.'[3] As Mach entered the bus, then, he believed with respect to Mach—and therefore with respect to himself—that he was a shabby pedagogue, but he did not believe *himself* to be a shabby pedagogue. The experience might have made him say: '*That* man is a shabby pedagogue'. But—prior to his discovery of the mirror—it would not have led him to say: '*I* am a shabby pedagogue'.

Examples are readily multiplied. Elizabeth Anscombe[4] has noted that it is one thing for Descartes to doubt the identity of *Descartes* with Descartes and quite another thing for him to doubt the identity of *himself* with Descartes. She also cites this example:

'When John Smith spoke of James Robinson he was speaking of his brother, but he did not know this.' That's a possible situation. So similarly is 'When John Smith spoke of John Horatio Auberon Smith (named in a will perhaps) he was speaking of himself, but he did not know this'. If so, then 'speaking of' or 'referring to' oneself is compatible with not knowing that the object one speaks of is onself.

Anscombe goes on to say that the expression: 'He doesn't realize the identity with himself' is not the 'ordinary' reflexive but 'a special one which can be explained only in terms of the first person'.

An abundance of other examples may be found in the writings of Peter Geach and Hector Castaneda, who brought this difficult problem before the attention of contemporary philosophy.[5]

To understand the 'he, himself' locution, let us consider its use in clauses expressing the objects of believing. We may contrast the three locutions:

(P) The tallest man believes that the tallest man is wise.
(Q) There is an x such that x is identical with the tallest man and x is believed by x to be wise.
(S) The tallest man believes that he himself is wise.

An alternative formulation of S would be: 'That tallest man believes himself to be wise'.

The distinction between P and Q is familiar: P is an example of belief *de dicto*; Q is an example of belief *de re*; and S is an example of the 'he, himself' locution in application to believing.

Let us consider, then, the logical relations among our three sentences. We may say:

(a)   P implies Q;

(b)   Q does not imply P.

(c)   S does not imply P;

(d)   P does not imply S;

(e)   S implies Q;

(f)   Q does not imply S.

Given our assumptions about *de re* belief, we may say that the only one of these assumptions that may seem problematic is the last one—that Q does not imply S. So, let us consider the conditions under which it might be the case that Q is true and S is false.

Assume, then, that S is false. In this case the tallest man cannot sincerely say: 'I believe that I am wise'. Suppose, however, that he reads the lines on his hand and takes them to be a sign of wisdom; he doesn't realize the hand is his; and he is unduly modest and entirely without conceit. He arrives at the belief, with respect to the man in question, that he is wise—just as I might arrive at the belief, with respect to you, that you are wise, and just as Mach had arrived at the belief, with respect to the man he was looking at, that that man was a shabby pedagogue. Hence, although the tallest man cannot sincerely say: 'I believe that I am wise', he can correctly express his conclusion by saying: 'Well, *that* person, at least, is wise'.

If we can say that P refers to a belief *de dicto* and Q to a belief *de re*, then we could say that the 'he, himself' locution, S, is an instance of belief *de re*, for S does imply Q.

The 'he, himself' locution, unlike the *de dicto* locution, implies the *de re* locution. Yet there is one respect in which the 'he, himself' locution is like belief *de dicto* and unlike belief *de re*. Using the 'he, himself' locution to contrast the three belief situations, we may note these things about what the believer can know: (i) If the tallest man believes *de re*, with respect to the tallest man, that he is wise, it may not be at all evident to him that he *does* thus believe with respect to the tallest man that he is wise (for he may have no idea that the man in question *is* the tallest man). (ii) If the tallest man believes *de dicto* that the tallest man is wise (that is to say, if the proposition that the tallest man is wise is one that he accepts), then it is *ipso facto* evident to him that he believes that the tallest man is wise. And, finally, (iii) if he believes that *he, himself* is wise, then it is also *ipso facto* evident to him that he believes that he, himself is wise. This last point might encourage one to say that such believing is, after all, a matter of accepting first-person propositions, but we cannot take this course if we decide that there are no such propositions.

Why is it that the ordinary quantifier and variables don't seem to suffice in the case of the 'he, himself' locution? Does our sentence S express some element of subjectivity that escapes the ordinary notation of quantification—some kind of inner connection or intimacy that we don't encounter when we are not dealing with the relation of the phsychological subject to itself?

Some Ways of Dealing with the Problem

At first consideration the problem may seem to admit of an easy solution. 'Can't we just say that if a person x believes *himself* to be wise, then x believes x to be wise and, moreover, x believes that he is x? In other words: 'There exists an x such that x believes x to be wise" tells us this: "There exists an x such that x believes that x is wise and he is x".'

But this, of course, is only to transfer the problem. Our new problem will be: What is the relation between 'There exists an x such that x believes that x is wise and *he* is x' and 'There exists an x such that x believes that x is wise and x is x'? A similar objection applies to 'There exists an x such that x believes that x is wise and x knows that he is x'.

What of 'There exists an x such that x believes x to be wise and x *knows who* x is'? But the tallest man may well have known who he was, just as Mach, when he saw himself in the mirror, knew who he was. Hence x can be such that (i) he knows who x is,

(ii) he believes x to be wise, and (iii) he does not believe himself to be wise.

What of 'There exists an x such that x believes x to be wise and x knows who it is that x believes to be wise'? Here, too, the two types of locution reappear: we must distinguish between 'x knows who it is that *he* believes to be wise' and 'x knows who it is that x believes to be wise'. And, once again, the two locutions are so related that the first implies the second, but not conversely.

Most recent philosophers who have considered the problem assume that the 'he, himself' locution can be explained only on the assumption that there are first-person propositions, and most such theorists are in agreement on two further points. Each theorist suggests that he can express his own first-person propositions by using the first-person pronoun, and each theorist seems to despair of being able to express any first-person proposition of any person other than himself.

Let us briefly consider four recent attempts to deal with the problem.

(i) There is Anscombe's theory, which she summarizes as follows: '"I am this thing here" is, then, a real proposition, but not a proposition of identity. It means: this thing here is the thing, the person . . . of whose action *this* idea of action is an idea, of whose movements *these* ideas of movement are ideas, of whose posture *this* is the idea.'[6] She thus attempts to explicate *her* use of the first-person pronoun in terms of the demonstrative 'this'. It is clear that she cannot explicate *my* use of 'I' in this way, and I think she might concede that she cannot grasp my 'I'-propositions at all. Indeed, how would we report her view if we did not have access to direct quotation? We would have to say something like this: According to Professor Anscombe, the proposition she expresses by saying: 'I am this thing here' says that the thing to which *she* is calling attention is the person whose action *her* present idea of action is an idea . . . and so on.

It is fair to say, therefore, that she does not have a general theory about the indirect reflexive. That is to say, she does not present a theory which illuminates the logical relations among our three sentences, P, Q and S.

(ii) As noted above, I had previously defended the view that, for each person, that person's use of 'I' is such that he is its referent and his individual essence or haecceity is its sense. I said, in effect, that 'Jones believes that he himself is wise' tells us this: 'Jones has an individual essence H; he accepts a proposition which is certain for him and necessarily such that it is true if and only if whatever has H is wise.'[7] I, too, suggested that no one is able to grasp the 'I'-propositions of any other person.

This view is plausible only if it is plausible to suppose that there are 'I'-propositions. And, as we have seen, the most plausible version of the thesis that there are 'I'-propositions presupposes that there are individual essences and that each person can readily grasp his own; but we are now sceptical about these presuppositions.

(iii) Castaneda also assumes that there are first-person propositions. He tells us that, when a person uses an 'I'-sentence, then he is expressing a first-person proposition which 'is different from every third-person proposition about him, and, of course, different from any third-person proposition about anything else'.[8] Castaneda thus seems to suggest the view that he could never express *my* 'I'-propositions, and I believe he would say that, strictly speaking, he could not even grasp them. He is led, moreover, to a special ontological view about first-person propositions. I had assumed, in the view set forth above, that first-person propositions are abstract objects which imply individual essences. Castaneda, however, is led to complicate the theory of propositions. He holds that first-person propositions, instead of being abstract objects, as propositions are commonly thought to be, are *contingent* things: 'the first-person propositions belonging to a person X have a contingent existence; they exist if and only if X exists'.[9]

One could go on to hold—but it is not clear whether Castaneda does this—that, for *every* contingent thing, there are contingent propositions that thus 'belong to' that thing—propositions which exist only if the thing exists. I believe that this view is intended by those philosophers who hold that, in addition to those propositions which are abstract objects, there are also contingent 'singular propositions', but we shall stay clear of these ontological complications.

(iv) Finally, making use of the concept of *de re* belief and the concept of empirical certainty, I once proposed a theory which does *not* presuppose that there are 'I'-propositions. Unfortunately, the theory is inadequate on other grounds.

THE PROBLEM OF FIRST PERSON SENTENCES

I had said that a proposition is *empirically certain* for a given subject S provided that the proposition is one that is (a) contingent, (b) such that accepting it is more reasonable for S than withholding it, and (c) there is no contingent proposition *i* such that accepting *i* is more reasonable for S than accepting the proposition in question. Then I said:

Propositions that are empirically certain, in this sense, will be propositions about what are traditionally called 'states of mind'—propositions about thinking, feeling, and believing. No proposition that is empirically certain for a given subject S will imply the existence of any person other than S. If I am not in pain, then the proposition *someone is in pain* cannot be empirically certain for me.[10]

I then went on to say that 'The tallest man believes that he himself is wise' could be put this way: 'It is empirically certain for the tallest man that there is someone who is believed to be wise'. The definition presupposed, as I said, that 'the proposition, *there is someone who is believed to be wise*, cannot be certain for any person unless that person can be said to believe that he, himself, is wise'. And then I was able to add:

The referent of the first-person expression 'I' in English is the speaker himself and the function of English expressions of the form: 'I am F', is to express the fact that it is empirically certain for the speaker that there is someone who is believed to be F.

This approach, I now realize, is subject to the following epistemological difficulty: we may say generally that, for any proposition or state of affairs p, if p has some positive epistemic status (say, that of being certain) for a given subject S, then it is possible to formulate an epistemic principle stating the conditions under which p has such positive status for S. The principle will say that, if those conditions obtain, then p has that status for S. The conditions in question will be describable without the use of epistemic terms. In other words, the principle would refer to some state or property of the subject which is necessarily such that, if the subject is in that state or has that property, then it is certain for that subject that there is someone who is believed to be wise.[11] But what state or property could thus render it certain for a given subject that *there is someone who is believed to be wise*? The properties of *being believed to be wise* and of *being such that there is someone one believes to be wise* will not suffice, for obviously one could have either of these properties without thereby being certain that there is someone one believes to be wise. The only property that would yield the desired certainty is that of *believing oneself to be wise*—but that property leaves us with our problem.[12]

An Approach to the Problem

Let us use the term 'emphatic reflexive' for the 'he, himself' locution such as S, and let us use 'non-emphatic reflexive' for those locutions such as Q that do not imply the 'he, himself', or emphatic, reflexive. Thus 'There exists an x such that x believes himself to be wise' (S) will express an emphatic reflexive, and 'There exists an x such that x believes x to be wise' (Q) will express a non-emphatic reflexive.

Perhaps it will be agreed that the distinction between the two types of reflexive is one that holds only in intentional or psychological contexts. Now there are two ways of interpreting the significance of this distinction. In either case, we ask: 'Why is it that the non-emphatic reflexive (for example, Q) does not imply the corresponding emphatic reflexive (for example, S)?' But in the one case, we would trace the failure of implication to certain peculiarities of the emphatic reflexive. We would try to exhibit the emphatic reflexive as a special case of the non-emphatic reflexive. Whereas in the other case, we would proceed in the opposite direction: we would try to exhibit the non-emphatic reflexive as a special case of the emphatic reflexive. If we take the second approach, we will deny that the emphatic reflexive presents us with any unique logical structure. We will say that the failure of implication is due, rather, to certain familiar facts about intentionality—as exhibited in the *non-emphatic* reflexive.

I suggest that, by exploring the possibility that the second approach is correct, we may arrive at a view enabling us to understand the logic of the two types of reflexive.

It will be instructive to remind ourselves of this fact: there are philosophers who (justifiably or unjustifiably) are not convinced of the validity of the distinction between the two types of reflexive; and what they are sceptical about is not the existence of the emphatic reflexive, but the existence of the non-emphatic reflexive—they doubt that there is a sense of 'There exists an x such that x believes x to be wise' that does *not* imply 'There exists an x such that x believes himself to be wise'. What is peculiar in the distinction, they might say, is the assumption that there is a reflexive which is *not* emphatic.

Consider, then, the possibility that, in the case of non-psychological reflexives, *all* reflexives are emphatic. In the case of motors, say, it will not matter whether we say: 'There is an x such that x refuels x' or: 'There is an x such that x refuels itself'; there is no non-emphatic reflexive here.

Indeed, we have here a kind of criterion of the psychological. If we can say: 'When the doctor treats the doctor, he thereby treats himself', then we are taking the verb, 'to treat' in a sense that is non-psychological or non-intentional. 'To treat' is here to be taken, wholly physicalistically, say as a matter of administering medicines and producing effects upon the patient. But if we can say: 'The doctor may treat the doctor without thereby treating *himself*', then we are taking the verb 'to treat' in a psychological or intentional sense. Treating, so interpreted, involves having certain beliefs and intentions that are directed upon the patient. If the doctor then treats the doctor and doesn't treat himself, then he is in the position Mach was in when he saw himself enter the bus. He is not only administering medicines and producing effects, but he also bears a certain intentional relation to himself. If we can specify what this relation is, then we may conclude that something psychological or intentional is involved when the non-emphatic reflexive holds and the emphatic reflexive fails.

So, instead of trying to understand the 'he, himself' locution as a special case of the ordinary *de re* locution, we shall try to understand the ordinary *de re* locution as a special case of the 'he, himself' locution.

If this, however, is the correct approach, then we have made a mistake in our formulation. We should have given S the ordinary quantification notation, and we should have exhibited Q as something that is obviously derivable from S. How are we to do this? We shall answer this question in the following chapter.

Notes

1 Compare Frege, 'The Thought: A Logical Inquiry', *Mind*, LXV (1956), pp. 289–311, and Husserl, *Logical Investigations* (London: Routledge and Kegan Paul, 1970), pp. 315–16. I defended this view in Chapter One of *Person and Object: A Metaphysical Study* (London and La Salle, Ill., Allen and Unwin, Ltd., and the Open Court Publishing Company, 1976).
2 See Franz Brentano, *Psychology from an Empirical Standpoint* (London: Routledge & Kegan Paul, 1973), pp. 311–15; and *Kategorienlehre* (Hamburg: Felix Meiner Verlaag, 1968), pp. 153–160.
3 Ernst Mach, *Analysis of Sensations* (Chicago: The Open Court Publishing Co., 1897), p. 4n. (Mach asked himself: 'Was steight doch da für ein herabgekommener Schulmeister ein?' Compare *Beiträge zur Analyse der Empfindungen* (Jena: Gustav Fischer, 1886), p. 34. I owe this reference to Michael Corrado.
4 Elizabeth Anscombe, 'The First Person', in S. Guttenplan, ed., *Mind and Language: Wolfson College Lectures 1974* (Oxford: The Clarendon Press, 1975), pp. 45–65.
5 Compare P. T. Geach, 'On Beliefs about Oneself' (1957), in *Logic Matters* (Oxford: Basil Blackwell, 1972), pp. 128–9. Compare the following by H. N. Castaneda: 'He: A Study in the Logic of Self-Consciousness', *Ratio*, Vol. 8 (1966), pp. 130–57; 'Indicators and Quasi-indicators, *American Philosophical Quarterly*, Vol. 4 (1967), pp. 85–100; 'On the Logic of Attributions of Self-Knowledge to Others', *The Journal of Philosophy*, Vol. 65 (1968), pp. 439–56, and 'On the Phenomeno-Logic of the I', *Akten des XIV. Internationalen Kongresses für Philosophie*, Vol. III (University of Vienna, 1969), pp. 260–6. See also John Perry, 'The Problem of the Essential Indexical', *Nous*, XIII (1979), pp. 3–21.
6 'The First Person', p. 61.
7 *Person and Object*, p. 37.
8 H. N. Castaneda, *Thinking and Doing: The philosophical Foundations of Institutions* (Dordrecht: D. Reidel Publishing Company, 1975), p. 159.
9 'On the Phenomeno-Logic of the I', p. 267.
10 See 'The Self and the World', in *Wittgenstein and His Impact on Contemporary Thought: Proceedings of the 2nd International Wittgenstein Symposium* (Vienna: Holder-Pichler-Tempsky, 1978), pp. 407–410. The quotations appear on p. 410.
11 Such principles will be discussed in detail in Chapters 7 and 8.
12 For a critical account of the relations between the two theories I had formerly held, compare Dieter Henrich, 'Zwei Theorien zur Verteidigung von Selbstvewusstsein', *Grazer Philosophische Studien*, VII (1979).

Chapter 4
INDIRECT ATTRIBUTION

A Re-examination of Intentional Attitudes

BELIEVING must be construed as a relation between a believer and *some* other thing; this much is essential to *any* theory of belief. What kind of thing, then? There are various possibilities: sentences, propositions or states of affairs, properties, individual things. The simplest conception, I suggest, is one which construes believing as a relation involving a believer and a property —a property which he may be said to attribute to himself. Then the various senses of believing may be understood by reference to this simple conception.

Analogous observations may be made with respect to other intentional attitudes—for example, desiring, knowing, hoping, intending. In each case, there is an elementary conception of the attitude in question in terms of which more familiar conceptions can be explicated. This elementary type of attitude, as we shall see, will enable us to understand the relation between the emphatic reflexive—the 'he, himself' locution—and the non-emphatic reflexive. It will throw light upon the nature of *de re* belief, as well as upon the use of proper names and such demonstratives as 'I', 'here' and 'this'.

I shall therefore suggest (1) that each of these intentional attitudes has a primary form which does not take a propositional object, and (2) that we may characterize the more familiar *de dicto* and *de re* forms of these attitudes in terms of the primary, non-propositional form.

I shall develop these points in their application to believing. But what I say may be applied, *mutatis mutandis*, to the other intentional attitudes.

Direct Attribution

Our basic doxastic locution may be spelled out as:

The property of being F is such that x directly attributes it to y.

The letter 'F' is schematic and may be replaced by any predicative expression having a property as its sense; for simplicity we omit reference to a particular time. Our undefined formula contains the two variables, 'x' and 'y', but we shall also affirm the following principle about the nature of direct attribution:

P1   For every x, every y and every z, if x directly attributes z to y, then x is identical with y.

We shall also assume that the *content* of attribution is always a *property*—and hence a property in the purified sense we set forth in Chapter II.

P2   For every x, every y and every z, if x directly attributes z to y, then z is a property.

The 'he himself' locution of the indirect reflexive may now be introduced as an abbreviation of our undefined locution.

D1 x believes that he himself is F = Df. The property of being F is such that x directly attributes it to x.

Let us consider, then, what is presupposed by our use of the concept of direct attribution.

We are assuming, Platonistically, that there *are* properties or attributes and that some of these properties or attributes are exemplified and some are not. Our basic locution, 'the property of being F is such that x directly attributes it to y', is intentional: the expression in the place of 'the property of being F' need not designate a property that is exemplified.

We presuppose two things about the abilities or faculties of believers. First, a believer can take himself as his intentional object; that is to say, he can direct his thoughts upon himself. And, secondly, in so doing, grasps or conceives a certain property which he attributes to himself. We also presuppose that he is able to grasp or conceive propositions or states of affairs.

All other reference can be explicated in terms of such presuppositions. What we have said about attribution and believing may be extended to the other intentional attitudes and, indeed, to thought itself. Let us consider the latter briefly.

The expression 'entertaining' is sometimes taken to refer to the generic sense of thinking. Entertainment is then recognized as being an intentional attitude taking the same *objects* as believing, but not involving the doxastic commitment that is essential to believing. H. H. Price has described it this way: 'The entertaining of propositions is the most familiar of all intellectual phenomena. It enters into every form of thinking and into many of our conative and emotional attitudes as well. Indeed, one might be inclined to say that it is the basic intellectual phenomenon; so fundamental that it admits of no explanation or analysis, but on the contrary all other forms of thinking have to be explained in terms of it'.[1] Price here assumes that believing is essentially propositional.

But if the primary form of believing is the direct attribution of a property to oneself, then the primary form of 'entertainment' is analogous. It is that phenomenon which is *considering* oneself as having a certain property—or, alternatively put, thinking of oneself as having a certain property. If I am trying to make a decision as to which direction to travel in, I consider myself as travelling in one direction and then consider myself as travelling in another. I will be the *object* of such considering and the property I consider myself as having will be the *content*.

Our principal concern, in the present book, is with belief, or attribution.

Indirect Attribution

Let us now return to our general question about intentionality or indirect reference: How does one succeed in making *other* things one's intentional objects? In other words, how is it possible to refer to individuals other than oneself?

For example, how do I make you my intentional object? I would say that the answer is this: I make you my object by attributing a certain property to myself. The property is one which, in some sense, singles you out and thus makes you the object of an *indirect* attribution. What would it be, then, for one of my properties to single you out?

The answer involves two points:

(1) There is a cerain relation R which is such that *you* are the thing to which I bear R. I shall say that such a relation is an *identifying relation*—a relation by means of which the believer

singles out the object of his indirect attribution. Thus you might be the person with whom I am talking, or the person I live across the street from, or the person I am sitting next to. (Note that, in saying that you are the thing that I bear the relation R to, I am not saying that I am *the* thing that bears R to you—or that you are the thing that bears R to me. If we use Russell's notation for descriptive functions, then, if I am x, you should be designated, not as 'the R of x', but as 'the thing that x bears R to'.)

(2) The property I directly attribute to myself may be said to imply that there is just one thing to which I hear R and that that thing has the property of being F. That is to say, the property is necessarily such that whatever has it bears R to just one thing and to a thing that is F.

When this situation obtains, I indirectly attribute to you the property of being F.

Suppose, for example, that I am talking with you and only with you, and that I believe with respect to you that you are wearing a hat. Then the property of being F—the property I indirectly attribute to you—would be that of wearing a hat; the identifying relation R that I bear to you and only to you would be that of talking with; and the property that I directly attribute to myself would be the property of talking with exactly one person and with a person wearing a hat. In thus indirectly attributing a property to you, I directly attribute a certain two-fold property to me. The first part of my direct attribution (that I bear the relation R to one and only one thing) will be correct; for I can attribute a property to you only if the identifying relation by means of which I attempt to single you out *is* a relation I bear to you and only to you. But the second part of the direct attribution (that the thing to which I bear R is a thing that is F) may or may not be correct. In either case, we may say: you are such that, *as* the person I am talking with, I indirectly attribute to you the property of wearing a hat.

More generally, whenever we have indirect attribution, then the believer attributes a property to the object, *as* the thing to which he bears a certain identifying relation. We may call the property thus attributed the *content* of the indirect attribution, and the thing to which the property is attributed the *object*. Thus the believer directly attributes to himself the property of bearing that identifying relation to a thing that exemplifies that content. Our definition of *indirect attribution*, then, is one that is suggestion by the proposed definition of *de re* belief mentioned at the beginning of the previous chapter. It is this:

D2 y is such that, as the thing that x bears R to, x indirectly attributes to it the property of being F = Df x bears R to y and only to y; and x directly attributes to x a property which entails the property of bearing R to just one thing and to a thing that is F.

One property or relation may be said to *entail* another property or relation provided the first is necessarily such that (a) if it is exemplified then the second is exemplified and (b) whoever conceives it conceives the second.

Given the definition just formulated, we may introduce the following abbreviated locution:

D3 y is such that x indirectly attributes to it the property of being F = Df. There is a relation R such that x indirectly attributes to y, as the thing to which x bears R, the property of being F.

According to this proposal, then, whenever a person indirectly attributes a property to a thing, he can specify a certain identifying relation R which is such that the thing in question is *the* thing to which he bears R. This is not difficult to do. Consider, for example, my beliefs about the present President of the United States. What relation R would be such that he is the thing to which I bear R? One would be that of living in the country where he is the President. Do we have here a *relation* such that Mr Carter is the thing to which I bear that relation? Surely we do. The relation is that expressed by: 'x lives in a country where the President of that country is identical with y'.

Consider another example. What identifying relation is such that W. V. Quine is now the thing to which I bear that relation? It could be that of looking at my copy of a certain book that he wrote ('x is looking at his copy of the book *The Ways of Paradox*, which was written by y').

If there is a relation R such that you can be said to be the one to whom I bear R, and if there is a further relation S such that some third thing can be said to be the thing to which you bear S, then I may be in a position to attribute something indirectly to that third thing; and so on *ad indefinitum*. For example, if you are the one with whom I am talking, if there is an automobile which is the automobile that belongs to you, and if there is a person who is now driving that automobile, then I may be in a position to attribute something indirectly to that person—i.e. to the person who is driving the automobile that belongs to the person with whom I am talking. Or, again, if a certain house happens to be the thing at which I am looking, if Jack is the person who built the house, if Mary is the person who is married to Jack, then Mary will be the person who is married to the person who built the house at which I am looking, and I may, therefore, attribute a property to Mary.

Here, then, we have a procedure for answering the question of Wittgenstein's which we began: 'What makes my idea of him an idea of *him*?', and we can answer it without appealing to words or to terms that refer to him. A partial answer would be this: 'There is a certain relation I bear just to him; and I directly attribute to myself the property of bearing that relation to just one thing'. It is difficult to think of any answer that is simpler than this.

But to the question: 'What makes his *direct* attribution of a property to himself an attribution of a property to *him*?' there can be no answer at all, beyond that of 'He just does—and that is the end of the matter!' Do we have here, then, a difficulty that is unique to the present theory? It is important to see that *every* theory of reference and intentionality is such that, at some point, it must provide a similar answer: 'It just does'. Thus, according to the propositional theory of belief, I make *me* my object by making certain propositions my object. And how do I make those propositions my object? The answer must be that I do this directly—and not via some other thing which I have made my object.

The definition of indirect attribution that I have proposed here is similar, in fundamental respects, to a definition arrived at independently by David Lewis. Lewis writes: 'A subject ascribes a property X to individual Y under description D if and only if (1) the subject bears the relation Z uniquely to Y, and (2) the subject self-ascribes the property of bearing relation Z uniquely to something which has the property X.' Lewis uses 'belief *de se*' for what I have called 'direct attribution'.

'Under a Description'

We can now make use of a locution similar to one that is a part of the active vocabulary of many contemporary philosophers: this is the 'under a description' locution. One could say, in connection with our example, that I indirectly attribute to you 'under the description, the person with whom I am talking' the property of wearing a hat. For this is to say only that I attribute this property to you *as* the person with whom I am talking. (It should be noted that I have not taken the 'under a description' locution as an undefined philosophical locution, but have defined it—in terms of what we have in D2 above.)

Suppose, then, that I indirectly attribute the property of wearing a hat to you under the description, the one with whom I am talking. It may well be that, 'under certain other descriptions' (say, as the one who robbed the bank where my savings are), I do not attribute this property to you—perhaps under that description I even attribute to you the property of *not* wearing a hat.

Indeed, it may be said more generally that, no matter how well I may be acquainted with you, it is possible that, although (1) I attribute a certain property to you under one of your descriptions, nevertheless (2) there is *another* description which is such that, under *that* description, I attribute the negation of the property in question to you.

Ordinarily, when we have occasion to say of one thing that it is thus believed about by some other thing, we do not specify the description under which the first thing is believed about by the second. But, I suggest, there always is such a description and it is usually made obvious by the context of utterance. (Not many will misunderstand you if, in reporting a masquerade ball in Washington, you say: 'I thought the President's wife was the Secretary of the Treasury'.)

I can make you the object of my direct attribution, then, whenever there is a description of you which is such that you can be believed about by me under that description. Shall we say, then, that you can be believed about by me whenever there is an identifying relation which is such that you are the thing to which I bear that relation?

We will answer this question when we discuss the problem of *de re* belief, in the final chapter.

Solution of the Problem of the 'He, Himself' Locution

Let us now return to the problem of the 'he, himself' locution which was set forth in the previous chapter. Consider once again the two sentences (S) 'The tallest man believes that he himself is wise' and (Q) 'There is an x such that x is identical with the tallest man and x is believed by x to be wise'. I had said that we should formulate S in the ordinary quantification notation and in a way that would illuminate the logical relation between S and Q. The notation should make clear, in particular, that although S implies Q, Q does not imply S.

I suggest, then, that what the sentences S and Q come to is the following:

S'   There is an x such that x is identical with the tallest man, and the property of being wise is such that x directly attributes it to x.

Q'   There is an x such that x is identical with the tallest man, and the property of being wise is one such that x directly or indirectly attributes it to x.

It is clear from our definitions that S' implies Q'; and we have no reason to believe that Q' implies S'. If this analysis is correct, we have made out the difference between what is asserted by the two sentences S and Q without modifying the theory of quantification or extending our ontology beyond individuals, properties and relations, and propositions or states of affairs.

Indeed, we may now affirm a more general thesis about intentionality. In application to believing, it is the thesis that one may attribute a property to oneself without *directly* attributing that property to oneself. *This* fact is the source of our philosophical perplexity.

Consider once again Ernst Mach and the omnibus. When Mach saw himself in the mirror without yet realizing that he was looking at himself, he attributed to himself the property of being a shabby-looking schoolmaster. But he did so *indirectly* and *not* directly.

Then there was the doctor who treated the doctor but didn't treat himself. I had said that the doctor who treats the doctor and doesn't treat himself does so in virtue of a certain intentional relation he bears to himself. We can now say what this relation is. It is that expressed by: 'x indirectly but not directly endeavours to treat x'. (As we have noted, what we say about attribution has its analogues for other intentional attitudes—and hence for trying and undertaking.)

Again, as Elizabeth Anscombe noted, it was one thing for Descartes to doubt the identity of *Descartes* with Descartes, and another thing for Descartes to doubt the identity of *himself* with Descartes. Possibly the first doubt was a doubt concerning an attribution that is not direct, or possibly the first doubt concerned a proposition—the proposition, say, that the philosopher called 'Descartes' is identical with the philosopher called 'Descartes'. But the second doubt, in any case, would have been a doubt pertaining to an attribution that is direct.

As for John Horatio Auberon Smith, when he spoke of himself without knowing that he was speaking of himself, he was expressing an attribution that was not direct and he had not made the corresponding direct attribution.

When, in Castaneda's example, the editor of *Soul* believes with respect to the editor of *Soul* that he is a millionaire, but does not believe that *he himself* is a millionaire, then the property of being a millionaire is one that he *indirectly* attributes to himself —i.e. to the editor of *Soul*.

Content and Object

'What is the *object* of direct attribution?' Using a traditional terminology we may say that, if something x believes something y to be wise, then y is the *object* of x's belief and the property of being wise is the *content* of x's belief. In the case of direct attribution as well as attribution generally, we shall say that the property attributed is the *content* of the attribution and that the thing *to* which the property is attributed is the *object* of the attribution. But there is no reason to suppose that there is still *another* thing, somehow involving both the individual thing and the property of being wise, which is properly called '*the* object' of direct attribution, this despite the fact that in such a case one can ask: 'And *what* is it that he believes?' For we have rejected the view that explicates attribution by reference to the acceptance of propositions.

I shall quote a statement of the distinction between *content* and *object* which A. N. Whitehead had made in the *Concept of Nature*. Whitehead had noted that a demonstrative phrase may function merely as a gesture without expressing any part of the content that the speaker wishes to convey and that descriptive phrases, which on some occasions may be used to express such content, may on other occasions be used purely demonstratively. He cites the following example:

Suppose that the expositor is in London, say in Regent's Park and in Bedford College, the great college which is situated in that park. He is speaking of the college hall and he says:
'This college building is commodious.'
The phrase 'this college building' is a demonstrative phrase. Now suppose the recipient answers:
'This is not a college building. It is the lion-house in the zoo.'
Then, provided that the expositor's original proposition has not been couched in elliptical phraseology, the expositor sticks to his original proposition when he replies,
'Anyhow, *it* is commodious.'
Note that the recipient's answer accepts the speculative demonstration of the phrase 'This college building'. He does not say: 'What do you mean?' He accepts the phrase as demonstrating an entity, but declares that same entity to be the lion-house in the zoo. In his reply, the expositor in his turn recognizes the success of his original gesture as a speculative demonstration, and waives the question of the suitability of its mode of suggestiveness with an 'anyhow'. But he is now in a position to repeat the original proposition with the aid of a demonstrative gesture robbed of any suggestiveness, suitable or unsuitable, by saying:
'*It* is commodious.'
The '*it*' of this final statement presupposes that thought has seized on the entity as a bare objective for consideration.[3]

According to what I have said, then, the *object* of direct attribution is always oneself. The object of *indirect* attribution is the thing to which one indirectly attributes a property. It may be oneself, but it need not be oneself. Moreover, indirect attribution may also have *multiple objects*. I may believe, with respect to two things, x and y, that x is larger than y. In this case, there will be two identifying relations, R and S, which are such that I bear R to x and only to x and I bear S to y and only to y. I will directly attribute to myself a property which is necessarily such that anything having it will be such that the thing to which it bears R is larger than the thing to which it bears S. The objects of indirect attribution may thus be multiplied *ad indefinitum*. In the final chapters we shall consider in more detail attribution involving a plurality of objects.

If, as I shall argue, all belief is reducible to direct attribution, there will be a sense in which we can say that the believing subject is the *primary object* of all belief, and analogously for the other intentional attitudes.

'But one cannot attribute anything to oneself unless one has an immediate apprehension of oneself—an apprehension enabling one to pick out the self from among all other things. And your view does not tell us *how* we thus succeed in picking out ourselves.'

The objection confuses direct and indirect attribution. For it presupposes that, in order to attribute a property to myself directly, I must be aware of the kind of identifying relation I bear to the subject of attribute when I attribute something to it indirectly.

Our view may throw some light upon the ancient doctrine according to which knowledge requires an identity between the knower and the object known. For we may say that the primary form of *reference* requires an identity between the one who refers and the thing to which he refers: one directly attributes a property to oneself. The primary object of knowing will be the knower and so, in one sense, the ancient doctrine is correct. But in knowing oneself, one may thereby indirectly attribute a property to something other than oneself.

Eternal Objects and Indirect Attribution

How does one refer to eternal objects—to such objects as properties, relations and states of affairs?

I have said that we presuppose two things about the abilities and faculties of believers. One is the ability to take oneself as an intentional object, and the other is the ability to conceive certain eternal objects. The primary way, then, of referring to an eternal object is to *conceive* it.

What is it to have a *belief* about an eternal object—say, a belief about the property blue? If we look to our formula for indirect attribution, we will say that one has a belief about the property blue provided that one indirectly attributes some further property to the property blue—considered *as* the thing to which one bears a certain relation. What kind of relation, then, might I bear to the property blue and only to the property blue? There are many possible relations, all involving the conception of the property blue. The property blue may be the only property I'm now conceiving, or it may be the only colour property I'm now conceiving, or it may be the only property I'm contrasting with the property green. In short, I may bear certain *intentional* relations to the property blue and only to the property blue.

If now I *believe* with respect to the property blue that, say, it can be exemplified by many different things, then I'm making an indirect attribution of the following sort: the property blue, *as* the property that I'm now conceiving (or the colour property I'm now conceiving, or the property I'm now contrasting with the property green) is such that I indirectly attribute to it the property of being capable of exemplification in many different things.

States of affairs and propositions are analogous. For they, too, are things that can be objects of conception, and one way to have a belief about such a thing is to attribute a property to it, once again *as* the thing one is conceiving in a certain way.

Does belief about eternal objects involve more than such indirect attribution? We shall return to this question in the final chapter, when we consider the nature of *de re* belief.

De Dicto Belief

How shall we characterize *de dicto* belief—that type of believing which consists in the acceptance of propositions or states of affairs?

It is more natural to speak of accepting 'propositions' than it is to speak of accepting 'states of affairs'. For the present, however, we shall use the expressions 'proposition' and 'state of affairs' interchangeably. In the *Appendix*, we shall note the sense in which propositions may be said to constitute a sub-species of states of affairs.

I propose this definition of *de dicto* belief:

D4 The state of affairs that p is accepted (*de dicto*) by x = Df. There is one and only one state of affairs which is the state of affairs that p; and either (a) x directly attributes to x the property of being such that p, or (b) x attributes to the state of affairs that p, as the thing he is conceiving in a certain way, the property of being true.

(In place of 'being true', we could also say 'obtaining'.) The letter '*p*' may here be replaced by any well-formed English indicative sentence, but we do not assume that every such sentence expresses a proposition or state of affairs. Hence our initial stipulation in the definiens above that there *is* the state of affairs that *p*.

The definition tells us, in effect, that there are two quite different conditions under which a person can be said to accept a proposition. The first condition is that wherein one attributes to oneself a certain universal property—that expressed by the locution, 'being such that *p*', and the second condition is that wherein one indirectly attributes to the state of affairs the property of obtaining (or being true). The first way of accepting a proposition is less sophisticated than the second since, unlike the second, it does not presuppose that the believer has the concept expressed by 'is true', or 'obtains'.

In reporting a person's *de dicto* belief, we do not need to use proper names, demonstratives or free variables in describing the content of his belief.

Let us now take note of an important fact about the logic of believing—more particularly, concerning the relation of direct attribution to belief *de dicto*. This fact constitutes a third principle about the logic of direct attribution.

P3 For any subject x, if x directly attributes to x the property of being F, and if x considers there being something that is F, then the proposition that something is F will be accepted by x.

One may be said to 'consider there being something that is F' if one conceives the proposition, *There being something that is F*, or if one conceives the property of being such that there is something that is F.[4] Our principle P3 above should be inteprreted as a necessary proposition pertaining to the nature of believing. It is necessary and *a priori* in just the sense in which such propositions as the following may be said to be necessary and *a priori*: for any subject S, if S accepts the proposition that it is raining and what is being sold on the market, then x accepts the proposition that wheat is being sold on the market.

One may ask concerning our principle: Why add the qualification: 'if x considers there being something that is F'? The answer is that it is possible for a person to believe himself, say to be

walking without having made the generalization to what is expressed by 'Something is walking'. But our principle tells us that, if one believes oneself to be walking and also conceives the proposition that someone is walking, or conceives the property of being such that someone is walking, then one will also believe, *de dicto*, that someone is walking.

Notes

1 H. H. Price, *Belief* (London: George Allen & Unwin, 1969), p. 192.
2 David Lewis, 'Attitudes *De Dicto* and *De Se*', *Philosophical Review*, LXXXVIII (1979), pp. 513–43. Earlier versions of my definition may be found in 'The Indirect Reflexive', in *Intention and Intentionality: Essays in Honour of G. E. M. Anscombe*, eds. Cora Diamond and Jenny Teichman (Brighton: The Harvester Press, 1979), pp. 39–53; and in 'Objects and Persons: Revision and Replies', in *Grazer Philosophische Studien*, Vol. 7/8 (1979), pp. 317–88. I am indebted to Allen Renear for criticisms of an earlier version of my definition.
3 A. N. Whitehead, *The Concept of Nature* (Cambridge: The University Press, 1930), pp. 6–7. Compare the distinction between the 'referential' and the 'attributive' uses of definite descriptions, in Keith Donnellan, 'Reference and Definite Descriptions', in H. Feigl, W. Sellars and K. Lehrer, eds., *New Readings in Philosophical Analysis* (New York: Appleton-Century-Crofts, 1972), pp. 59–71; the paper first appeared in 1966.
4 From the fact that there is the proposition, *There being something that is E*, it does *not* follow that there is the property of being such that there is something that is F. Properties, we have said, are necessarily such that they can be exemplified. Hence if the proposition expressed by 'There are round squares, is an impossible proposition, there will be no property expressed by 'being such that there are round squares'.

Chapter 5

THE INTERPRETATION OF DEMONSTRATIVES

The Interpretation of 'I'-sentences

WE are now in a position to consider the use of the first person pronoun and other demonstratives. We shall proceed upon the assumption that the primary function of such words is that of indicating the *object* of attribution. In thus saying that a certain use is the 'primary use' of a given expression, I mean that it is a use of the expression in terms of which all its other uses can be explicated.

In the present chapter, we presuppose the concepts of the *sense* and the *reference* of words and other linguistic expressions. In the following chapter, we shall suggest how such sense and reference may be explicated in terms of intentionality—in terms of the psychological states of those who use the language.

Let us begin by contrasting the English *sentences* 'I am standing' and 'Someone is standing' (or 'There is someone standing who is standing'). It is clear that 'I am standing' implies 'Someone is standing', but not conversely. Hence we may ask what it is that the first sentence tells us that the second does not.

Our two sentences are comparable to 'There are red horses' and 'There are horses': the first may be said to imply the second, but not conversely. In the case of 'There are red horses' and 'There are horses', we can explicate the logical relations between the two *sentences* by reference to the logical relations between the two *propositions* that the sentences express: the proposition expressed by the first sentence logically implies the proposition expressed by the second sentence. We are not, however, in a position to explicate the relation between 'I am standing' and 'Someone is standing' in this way, for we have withheld commitment with respect to the existence of 'first-person propositions'. Hence we cannot distinguish the two cases by saying that 'I am standing' expresses a proposition that is not expressed by 'Someone is standing'. How, then, are the two sentences related?

Let us consider the type of sentence we obtain if we existentially generalize upon a sentence of the form 'I am F', thus deriving a sentence of the form 'Something is F'. I think we may say of any such existential sentence that, if the expression replacing the latter 'F' has a property as its sense, then the sentence *does* express a proposition. One way, then, of explicating the use of such generalized sentences is to say this:

> The locution 'Something is F' has as its primary use in English that of expressing the following property of its utterer: accepting the proposition that something is F.

Let us note that the letter 'F' is here schematic and may be replaced by any predicative expression, and the word 'express', in its present use, must be distinguished from that use of 'express' which would enable us to say that 'Something is red' expresses the property of being red.

The concept of *expression* that we have singled out here is essential to the theory of language—or, at least, it is essential to any theory of language that is based upon what I have called the primacy of the intentional. Thus, in place of 'is used to express', we could say, more accurately, 'has as its primary use that of expressing'.[1]

One could abbreviate the above formula by saying that 'Something is F' is used in English to express the proposition that something is F, but the longer formula is preferable in that it is applicable in situations where what is expressed is something other than a proposition.

What, now, of the first-person pronoun? I shall speak just of the first-person pronoun in English; but what I say is readily adaptable to other languages, including those in which verbal forms take the place of personal pronouns. I suggest that the English sentence 'I am standing' expresses the speaker's property of being an x such that x directly attributes to x the property of standing—in other words, the property of being an x such that x believes himself to be standing. Hence, we may say more generally:

> The locution 'I am F' has as its primary use in English that of expressing the following property of its utterer: directly attributing the property of being F to itself.

We could also replace the final clause by: 'that of believing himself to be F.'

We have said that direct attribution is necessarily such that, for every x and y, if x directly attributes something to y then x is identical with y. Hence we may say that each of us has a kind of privileged access to himself: each person is such that he can directly attribute properties to himself and he cannot directly attribute anything to anything *other* than himself. This privileged access is thus associated with the use of the first-person pronoun. It should, however, be emphasized that we have *not* explicated such access—as so many philosophers do—by reference to the use of the first-person pronoun. In accord with our principle of the primacy of the intentional, we have explicated the use of the first-person pronoun—and privileged access—by reference to direct attribution.

Statements about Oneself

We have spoken of the *English* locution 'I am F.' We may now extend our analysis generally to statements about oneself without restricting ourselves to any particular language or to languages containing personal pronouns. Let us say:

x says that he himself is F = Df. x utters in a certain language something which is such that its primary use in that language is that of expressing the following property of its utterer: believing himself to be F.

We could, then, simplify our account of the use of 'I am F':

The locution: 'I am F' has as its primary use in English that of expressing the following property of its utterer: saying that he himself is F.

There are several objections that may occur to one at this point —especially if one is inclined to think of believing as being primarily propositional in content. The present view will become clearer if we consider three such objections:

(1) 'What is expressed by the sentence "I am F" may be true or false. How can this be if the sentence does not express a

proposition?' The answer is that, so far as the truth—or falsity—of what is expressed by 'I am F' is concerned, we may say simply this: 'I am F' is used *with truth* in English if and only if its utterer *is F*. We must distinguish truth from sincerity in this context. An expression is used *with sincerity* in a given language if and only if the property of its utterer that it is used in that language to express is one that its utterer believes himself to have. (We may note, in passing, that if the present account is accurate, the statement 'I am lying' may *not* be interpreted as 'The *proposition* I am asserting is false'.)

(2) '*What* one says, when one says "I am F", certainly stands in logical relations to various propositions. For example, as you have noted, the locution "I am F" logically implies the locution "Someone is F"—and you have also said that the latter locution normally does express a proposition. What is the nature of this logical relationship, then, if the one locution expresses a proposition and the other does not?'

Given what we have said about the truth of 'I am F', we see that it is impossible for 'I am F' to be used with truth in English unless there is something that is F. And so one could say that the locution 'I am F' implies the locution 'Something is F'.

(3) 'A well-formed sentence such as "I am wise" expresses a complete thought, and it couldn't be said to express a complete thought if there is no proposition which constitutes its meaning or sense.' The conclusion is simply a *non sequitur*. To attribute a property to oneself is to have a 'complete thought'; and 'I am wise' expresses the fact that the speaker attributes wisdom to himself.

And so we may say, as Anscombe does, that 'if Y makes assertions with "I" as subject, then those assertions will be true if and only if the predicates used thus assertively are true of x'.[2] But where she has attempted to explicate the 'he, himself' locution in terms of the use of the first person pronoun, the present account, if it is adequate, is an explication of the use of the first-person pronoun in terms of that intentional attitude that I have called 'direct attribution'—the attitude that we express by means of the 'he, himself' locution.

We can thus say of the first-person pronoun that it is used to designate the person who uses it. He uses it to single out what we have called the *object* of direct attribution. He does not use it to express any part of the *content* of that attribution.

The person who uses the first-person pronoun may be said to be its *referent* or *designatum*. But, given what we have said about first-person propositions and about direct attribution, we will not say that the first-person pronoun has a *sense*. In other words, we will not say of the first-person pronoun that there is a property constituting its sense or intention. (The term 'sense' will be considered in more detail in the following chapter.) For in directly attributing a property to oneself one need not thereby single out an *identifying* property of oneself. We shall return to this matter below.

We are now in a position to consider the problem formulated at the beginning of this chapter. The sentence 'I am standing' implies the sentence 'Someone is standing', but not conversely. How are we to interpret this fact if we are not to say that that the first sentence expresses a proposition which implies a property that is not implied by the second sentence? The proper explanation is this: the first sentence expresses the direct attribution of a certain property to oneself (in our example, the property of standing); and the second sentence expresses a proposition which is necessarily such that (i) it is true if and only if the property in question is exemplified and (ii) it is accepted by anyone who directly attributes that property to himself.

'I' and 'This'

We may now relate what we have said about the 'I' to other demonstratives. We shall be guided by the thought that the primary function of most demonstratives is that of indicating the *object* of attribution and *not* that of expressing the *content* of attribution. But where the primary use of 'I' is that of indicating the object of *direct* attribution, the primary use of such demonstratives as 'this' and 'that' is that of indicating the object of *indirect* attribution.

One may, of course, *define* some demonstratives in terms of others. Thus Russell once wrote: 'All egocentric words can be defined in terms of "this". Thus: "I" means "The biography to which this belongs"; "here" means "The place of this"; "now" means "The time of this"; and so on'.[3] Others might say, in the same spirit, that 'I' means 'The one who is making this utterance', and Elizabeth Anscombe has suggested still another way in which 'I' might be explicated in terms of 'this'. She writes:

'I am this thing here' is, then, a real proposition, but not a proposition of identity. It means: this thing here is the thing, the person . . . of whose action *this* idea of action is an idea, of whose movements *these* ideas of movement are ideas, of whose posture *this* is the idea.[4]

She thus attempts to explicate *her* use of the first-person pronoun in terms of 'this'. It is clear, however, that she cannot explicate *my* use—or your use—of the first-person pronoun in this way.

We, however, have explicated the use of the first-person pronoun in terms of direct attribution and without reference to the use of *other* demonstratives, and without presupposing that 'I' has a sense. We can explicate the use of other demonstratives in a similar way—and without explicating all of them by reference to the first-person pronoun.

Thus one use of 'this' may be explicated as follows:

'This thing is F' is used in English to express the following property of its utterer: believing himself to be such that the thing he is calling attention to is F.

Hence 'This thing is F' may be said to express a certain indirect attribution. The analysis does not presuppose that there is an 'indexical property' which constitutes the sense of the expression 'this thing'.

David Kaplan notes that there are conditions under which it might be informative for you if I were to say: 'That [pointing to Venus in the morning sky] is identical with that [pointing to Venus in the evening sky]'.[5] (He adds that 'I would of course have to speak very slowly'.) *What* would you thus learn? I might have expressed myself by saying: 'The thing I'm calling your attention to is identical with the thing I'm calling your attention to'. But, one may object, '*That* is hardly an informative sentence'! The objection overlooks the fact that the utterance takes time. What you know, when the utterance has finally been completed, is that the thing to which I most recently called your attention is identical with the thing to which I called your attention just before that. We have here a typical case of indirect attribution. You attribute to yourself—correctly and with evidence—a property H of the following sort: there is a relation R such that you bear R only to me; and H is necessarily such that, for every z, z has H, if and only if, z bears R to just one thing and to a thing x which is such that the last thing to which x called z's attention is identical with the next to the last thing to which x called z's attention.

We may distinguish the 'speaker's meaning' of a demonstrative from the 'hearer's meaning'. Thus the speaker's meaning of the demonstrative 'this' will be suggested by 'the thing to which I am calling attention', a phrase having as its sense a certain identifying relation which the speaker believes he bears to something. And the hearer's meaning will be suggested by 'the thing to which the person whom I hear speaking is calling attention' or—on occasion—by 'the thing to which the person whom I hear speaking is *undertaking* to call attention'. We may compare Husserl's observation: 'If someone says "this", he does not directly arouse in the hearer the idea of what he means, but in the first place the idea or belief that he means something lying within his intuitive or thought-horizon, something he wishes to point out to the hearer'.[6]

What, then, of the meaning of the first-person pronoun? I have said that, in English, the locution 'I am F' is used to express the speaker's direct attribution to himself of the property of being F. *My* use of the word 'I' may have a meaning for you, since I am the one who wrote the lines that you are reading. But my use of 'I' does not normally have a meaning for me: it does not have what we have called a speaker's meaning. And I suggest that 'I' is the only singular term of which this can be said.[7]

We may also say that, just as one of the primary uses of 'this' is involved in singling out the speaker's object, one of the primary uses of 'that' is involved in singling out the hearer's object. The speaker's meaning of 'that' will be suggested by 'the thing I have succeeded in bringing to your attention', and the hearer's meaning by 'the thing that the one who is addressing me is undertaking to bring to my attention'.

One significant difference between the use of the first person and the use of other demonstratives lies in this fact: The speaker is guaranteed that, in his use, the first-person pronoun does have an *object*—or designatum. But there is no such guarantee in the case of other demonstratives—with the possible exceptions of 'here' and 'now'. One may use 'this', for example, in the mistaken belief that there is something that it designates.[8]

Some Other Demonstratives

Consider 'here' and 'there'. Jones may have said, while in Chicago, 'It is cold here', and we may subsequently report his statement by saying: 'When Jones was in Chicago, he thought it was cold there'. That he was *in Chicago* may have had no part of the content of his belief. One way, then, of rendering our account of what he said would be this: 'When Jones was in Chicago, he thought he was in a place that is cold.'

This applies also to the use of 'here' in a principal clause. Thus we might say, in accordance with our 'I am F' formula above:

> 'Something here is F' has as its primary use in English that of expressing the following property of its utterer: being an x such that x believes himself to be in a place where something is F.

In using the word 'place', I do not mean to commit myself to an absolute theory of space. Places are such things as planets, countries, cities, pieces of property, and rooms.

'Here' and 'the place where I am' have the same speaker's meaning. But, as Godfrey Vesey points out, if you ask me where I am and I reply by saying: 'Here', I haven't thereby *told* you where I am,[9] and the reason for this is that I cannot be said to *tell you* where I am until I have given you information of another sort. It should enable you to relate yourself uniquely to the place where I am and to do so without reference to the fact that *I* am there.

One use of the word 'there', analogously, is that of indicating the place where the hearer or receiver is.

What of 'you'? I suggest that 'You are F', when 'you' is taken in the singular, may be interpreted as expressing the speaker's indirect attribution of the property of being F to the one he is addressing. I have said that 'I' is the only singular term that has no speaker's meaning. We might say, analogously, that 'you' is the only singular term that has no hearer's meaning, but it would be more nearly accurate to say that 'you' is the only singular term that has no *addressee's* meaning. 'You' could have a hearer's meaning for one who overheard a conversation.

'But', one may object, 'the locution: "*You* are the person I am addressing" may on occasion be highly informative for the one who is being addressed, and this would hardly be the case if it expresses no more than what is expressed by: "The person I am addressing is the person I am addressing".'

I suggest that, if we consider any occasion on which the statement: 'You are the person I am addressing', is informative, we will find that a more accurate statement would have been: 'You are the person I *was* addressing'. Consider the dialogue: 'Please step forward'. 'Who is it that you are talking to?' 'I'm talking to you.' Is this counter to what I have said? I think not, for I believe that a more accurate formulation of the dialogue would have been something like this: 'Please step forward.' 'Who was it that you were talking to when you said that?' 'I was talking to you.'

Given an explication of the uses of 'you' and of 'I', do we have, *ipso facto*, an explication of some of the uses of 'we'? But we should not suppose that 'We are F' is always equivalent to the conjunction of 'You are F' and 'I am F.' Consider such sentences as : 'We are a party of six' and 'We are much more effective together than alone'. But these uses of 'we'—like the imperial use of 'we'—involve no interesting questions of principle.

Temporal Demonstratives

Most temporal demonstratives—'today', 'tomorrow', 'yesterday', 'next year', 'last week'—can be explicated in obvious ways by reference to 'now'. What, then, of 'now'? What am I expressing, for example, if I say 'It is now raining'? Many philosophers, unfortunately, seem to believe that the word 'now' has an attributive *sense* in each of its uses (a different one for each time that it is used) and that this sense constitutes an identifying property enabling us to single out the time *at* which 'now' is uttered. But what is this property? Is it an identifying mark comparable to a label on which a date is written? Surely times don't come thus labelled with dates or with any other identifying properties. One can't look the time over and conclude, say, that it is 4:23 pm, Eastern Standard Time, November 16, 1969 AD.

Some would try to explicate 'now' in terms of 'this'. As our quotation from Russell suggests, one might say, pointing, 'Now is the time of this', and thus presupposing that there is one and only one time which is properly called '*the* time of this'. If what I have said is true, however, 'this' is to be explicated in terms of the first person. So 'Now is the time of this' would become: 'Now is the time of the thing to which I am calling attention'. Let us consider, then, this new statement.

Must we be more explicit and say: 'Now is the time of the thing to which I am *now* calling attention'? If we must, then the explication is circular, and in fact it would seem that we *need* not insert 'now' into our explication. The reason we need not insert it is that our sentence is in the present tense and is therefore such that the insertion of 'now' in it would be redundant. But if the occurrence of 'now' is redundant in that sentence, then it would also be redundant in our original sentence: 'It is now raining'.

To understand temporal demonstratives, we must take tense seriously. Thus 'It is now raining' says no more nor less than 'It is raining'. Is 'now', then, always redundant?

It has been pointed out that when 'now' is within the scope of an intentional operator, as in 'The weatherman said that it would be raining now', then its use is not redundant, for removal of 'now' alters the content of what has been said.[10] Yet even here 'now' is redundant in the following respect: the sentence could be paraphrased without using 'now' or any synonym.

Consider 'The weatherman had said that it would be raining now'. Perhaps we could put this by saying: 'The weatherman had made a prediction which was true if and only if it is raining'. But this type of paraphrase may not do justice in every case to the actual *content* of the earlier prediction. Suppose that the weatherman had said three days ago, 'In three days it will be raining'. It is natural to report his belief by saying: 'Three days ago he thought that it would be raining *now*'. Can we put this without using 'now' or a synonym? We could say: 'Three days ago, he attributed to himself the property of being such that it will rain in three days'. (If he thought that it was raining then, we could say: 'Three days ago he attributed to himself the property of being such that it *is* raining', but we should *not* say: 'Three days ago he attributed to himself the property of being such that it is raining *now*'. For the demonstrative 'now', in such contexts, retains its connection with the present, but the present tense in such contexts does not retain its connection with the present. Thus we may say without ambiguity: 'The property of being such that it *is* walking *was* had by everything that has ever walked and *will be* had by everything that ever will walk'.)

Consider another type of example. I might say to you, while hiking, 'Our friends thought that we would be tired by now'. In this case, I might mean that we are at a certain point in our hike which is such that our friends believed, with respect to that point, that when we received it we would be tired. In this use, 'He believed that so-and-so would happen now' may be explicated this way: 'There is an event e such that he believed so-and-so would occur when e occurs; and e is occurring'.

Any adequate theory of time should provide an interpretation for the locution: 'There is a time t such that . . .' But if we take tense seriously, we will distinguish *now*—the present time—from all other times in one or the other of two different ways. We could say, on the one hand, that the present time is the only time that *does* exist—all other times being such that either they *did* exist or they will *exist*. Or we could say, as I shall suggest in the *Appendix* to this book, that times are a certain sub-species of states of affairs and that, like states of affairs, they are such that either they obtain or they do not obtain. In the latter case, the present time would be the time that *is obtaining*, past times would be the times that *did obtain*, and future time would be those that *will obtain*. Although I assume that this second alternative is the correct one, what I shall say is readily adapted to the first.[11]

I have just said that the present time is the only time that is obtaining. *This* fact, surely, cannot be put without using 'now' or a synonym, and so 'now' and its synonyms are not completely redundant after all. Must we face the question, then, 'How do we single out and recognize the present time'?

In knowing that it is raining, I am in a position to know that the present time—the time that is obtaining—is a time *at* which it is raining. How can this be? The answer is, as I have said, that times are to be viewed as conjunctions of events or states of affairs. Oversimplifying what we shall put more precisely in the *Appendix*, we may say that the present time is a certain minimal conjunction of all those states of affairs that are obtaining. To say of an state of affairs or event that it occurs *at* the present time is to say, of it, that it is one of the events that are occurring, and we can arrive at *that* conclusion without singling out any identifying property of the present moment.

Let us consider the word 'then'. What are we to say of the sentence: 'At two o'clock he believed that it was then four o'clock?'[12] Clearly 'then'—in *this* use—is also redundant. For what we are saying is simply: 'At two o'clock he believed it was four o'clock'. (At two o'clock he directly attributed to himself the property of being such that it was four o'clock.)

Consider, then, a variant upon our earlier example: 'The day before yesterday I thought it was going to rain yesterday'. Here we must consider two different properties. One is the property of *believing that it is going to rain in one day*—a property that one has whenever one predicts rain for the following day. (Note that we have used the present tense in expressing the property; but we have not used 'now' or 'the present time'.) The second property is that of being such that one had the first property two days ago; i.e., it is the property of being such that two days ago one had the property of believing that it is going to rain in two days. This is the property I directly attribute to myself when I say: 'The day before yesterday I thought it was going to rain yesterday'.

In the final chapter, we shall consider more complex statements in which temporal and other demonstratives are related in various ways.

We next consider the sense and reference of proper names.

Notes

1 An alternative locution would be: 'is used to purport to express'. This latter might be more nearly adequate in describing the liar, since a liar is one whose words merely *purport* to express what he believes.
2 'The First Person', p. 55.
3 Bertrand Russell, *An Inquiry into Meaning and Truth* (New York: W. W. Norton & Company, 1940), p. 134.
4 'The First Person', p. 61.
5 In a mimeographed manuscript entitled *Demonstratives: An Essay on the Semantics, Logic, Metaphysics and Epistemology of Demonstratives and other Indexicals*, written in March, 1977. The example appears on p. 37.
6 E. Husserl, *Logical Investigations*, Vol. I (London: Routledge & Kegan Paul, 1970), pp. 316–17.
7 Using David Kaplan's terminology, we could say that 'I' is the only demonstrative that is 'directly referential'; all other demonstratives point to their referent via the meaning that they have on the occasion of their use. Kaplan introduces this terminology in *Demonstratives*. Kaplan's approach is different from that of the present work, since he presupposes that there are indexical properties and singular propositions and that all demonstrative reference is via such propositions.
8 Many logicians who have written about demonstratives do not provide for the possibility of there being such unsuccessful demonstration—we might call it

'mistaken indication'. An exception is Arthur Burkes: see his 'Icon, Index, and Symbol', *Philosophy and Phenomenological Research*, IX (1949), pp. 673–689; see especially pp. 688–9.
9   See Godfrey Vesey, *Personal Identity* (London: Macmillan, 1974), pp. 23–4.
10   See Hans Kamp, 'Formal Properties of "Now"', *Theoria*, XXXVII (1971); compare Arthur Prior, '"Now"', *Nous*, II (1968), pp. 101–9.
11   The first is defended by Nicholas Wolterstorff, in 'Can Ontology do without Events?', *Grazer Philosophische Studien*, VII (1979).
12   Evidently it was Robert Sleigh who first noted that such sentences have the characteristics of the 'he, himself' locution. See Hector-Neri Castaneda, 'Indicators and Quasi-Indicators,' *American Philosophical Quarterly*, IV (1967), pp. 85–100: see the second footnote of that article.

Chapter 6

ON THE MEANING OF PROPER NAMES

A Fallacy Involving Proper Names

WHAT we have said about the meaning of the first-person pronoun and of the demonstrative expressions that are closely associated with it should help us to evaluate the following philosophical argument about proper names:

'(i) The English sentence "Tom is standing" tells us considerably more than does the English sentence "Someone is standing", for the first cannot be true unless the second is true, but the second can be true even though the first is false. Thus the two sentences are related in the same way as are "A dog is standing" and "Something is standing". Therefore (ii) the proposition expressed by "Tom is standing" implies the proposition expressed by "Someone is standing", and not conversely. Now (iii) if two propositions are so related that the one implies the other but not conversely, and if the first of them implies some non-universal property, then it implies a non-universal property that the second does not imply. (A proposition may be said to imply a property if the proposition is necessarily such that if it is true then something has the property.) Thus the proposition that a dog is standing, unlike the proposition that something is standing, implies the property of being a dog. Hence (iv) the proposition expressed by "Tom is standing" implies a property that is not implied by the proposition expressed by "Someone is standing". Now (v) it can only be in virtue of the proper name "Tom" that the first sentence but not the second is associated with the property in question. Hence (vi) it is plausible to suppose that this property constitutes the *sense* of the proper name "Tom", and the most likely candidate for such a property would be that of *being identical with Tom*—a property which, surely, constitutes the individual essence of Tom.'

If what we have said about propositions and properties is correct, then the second step of the argument is mistaken. There is no *property* corresponding to the English expression, 'being identical with Tom', and therefore there is no *proposition* expressed by the English sentence 'Tom is standing'.

Since the reasoning is so common and since I believe it to be fallacious and metaphysically pernicious, I shall call it 'the proper name fallacy'. the fallacy involves several steps.

One begins by supposing that there is a propositional entity corresponding to every indicative sentence in which a proper name is used. One then draws a conclusion about the relation of the proper name to the proposition that is thus expressed. One concludes that the function of the proper name in a sentence such as 'Tom is standing' is that of expressing a part of the propositional *content* that is believed. Perhaps one will then go on to argue that, in a certain technical sense of the term 'sense', every proper name has a *sense*, and that this sense consists in some identifying property of the referent of the name—possibly its individual essence.

But if an identifying property is a property that only one thing can have at a time, and if properties are 'pure' in the sense we have described, then it is likely that, in the cases of most of the proper names in our language, one will look in vain for the identifying properties that are thus supposed to constitute their senses.

Alvin Plantinga has written: '. . . if I know such a proposition as *that person is elegantly attired*, I know a proposition entailing someone's essence'.[1] But if, as we are now assuming, all properties are pure or qualitative and if all states of affairs or propositions are abstract or eternal objects, then there is *no* state of affairs or proposition expressed by the sentence: 'That man is elegantly attired'. (Plantinga asks: 'Does *Socrates is wise* exist in worlds in which Socrates does not exist'? Our present response would be: it doesn't even exist even in those worlds in which Socrates *does* exist.) We are assuming, more generally, that although some sentences (e.g., 'The tallest man is wise') express propositions or states of affairs, the primary function of sentences containing demonstratives, indexicals or proper names is *not* that of expressing propositions or states of affairs.

All this presupposes that most declarative sentences are not used to express propositions: they express attribution rather than propositional acceptance. The *object* of the attribution which is thus expressed is, of course, a function of the context in which the sentence is uttered. (And we should note that, on those occasions when we are concerned to express *propositions*, the proposition that we express by a given sentence is almost never dependent upon the context of utterance. For, I would say, we express propositions only when we say such things as: 'All men are mortal'. 'There are mountains' and 'Two and two are four', thus using no demonstratives or proper names.)

What, then, is the function of proper names?

The Primary Function of Proper Names

The use of proper names, like that of demonstratives, is to be explicated in terms of our distinction between *object* and *content* —in so far as this distinction applies to indirect attribution. Consider again the English sentence: 'Tom is standing'. Speaking very roughly, we may say that the primary function of the proper name 'Tom' in this sentence is referential: it is that of directing the listener's attention to the *object* of the speaker's attribution. And this means, contrary to what is believed by those who commit the proper name fallacy, that the function of a proper name need not be that of expressing the *content* of attribution. But the primary function of the *predicative* expression 'is standing' is not referential but attributive: it is that of expressing the *content* of attribution.[2] Here, then, we have the primary function of proper names and the primary function of predicative expressions.

When I wish to convey my indirect attributions to you, I will want you to be able to do two things. One is to single out my *object*: that is to say, I will want you to find some relation P such that my object is the thing to which you bear R. If I succeed in doing this first thing I will have *demonstrated* or *indicated* my object for you. Secondly, I will want you to know the *content* of my assertion—that is to say, I will want you to know *what* it is that I am attributing to the object that I have indicated. And, thirdly, in the normal course of things, I would want you to attribute this content to the same object—however you may identify that object. (But, although I thus want to accomplish these different things, it may not be necessary for me to perform several different acts; and if I use written signs, it may not be necessary for me to use one sign to perform the one task and another sign to perform the other.)

Of course, I may be mistaken in thinking I bear the relation in question to just one thing. In such a case my demonstration will be unsuccessful, for my demonstrative expression will have no referent. (We will return to this matter below.)

If I succeed in conveying my belief to you, then I will have succeeded in getting you to single out my object. It is possible, of course, that you will single out the object in very much the same way as I do. Thus some of us may single out the President of the United States by means of the same identifying relation ('x lives in a country where the head of state is identical with v'). The President is the only thing to which I bear that relation—the only thing which is such that I live in the country where it is head of state. Some people might even identify the President in relation to me or to some other American. Thus you could identify him as the only thing which is such that the person whose lecture you are hearing lives in the country where it is head of state. Or again, you might single out the object via my identification of it—say, as 'the thing to which the one I am listening to is trying to call attention'. In this case, if my object is the thing to which I bear a certain relation B, and if I am the thing to which I bear a certain relation S, then your object might be singled out by you as the thing which is born R to by the thing to which you hear S. But, as we shall illustrate below, the way in which you single out the object *need* not involve me and it may be quite different from the way in which *I* single out the object.

Do Proper Names have Senses?

I have said that the primary use of a proper name in our ordinary language is purely referential: it is that of singling out an object and *not* that of expressing a content that is to be attributed to that object. Does this mean that proper names do not have senses?

The answer depends, of course, upon how we interpret the technical term 'sense'. More often than not, the term 'sense' as it is used by philosophers of language is taken very rigidly in what I shall call the *attributive sense* of the term 'sense'. We could say that the property of being F is the attributive sense of the term T in a language L, provided the following conditions hold: L is necessarily such that (i) for every x, T designates x in L if and only if x has the property of being F and (ii) for every y, if y uses T in L, then y conceives the property of being F.

Given this rigid interpretation of the term 'sense', we would have to say that the sense of a proper name (say, the proper name 'Tom') would be some identifying property of the bearer of the same (say, the property of being identical with Tom—if there *were* such a property). Now if what we have said about properties is correct, we cannot cite *any* identifying properties in the case of most of the individual things for which we have proper names. I would be sceptical, then, with respect to the supposition that proper names have attributive senses—in the rigid sense just defined.

If we say that proper names do not thus have attributive senses, should we conclude that proper names have meaning only to the extent that they denote or have a reference? This would certainly be a mistake. After all, one may ask, *how* could names and other demonstrative expressions perform their designative function if they do not have any meaning at all? And how would it be possible for us to interpret the uses of sentences containing proper names for objects that do not exist ('She was possessed by Beelzebub')? One may use a proper name in the mistaken belief that there *is* something that the name designates; in such a case we may say—to use Quine's expression—that the name at least *purports* to designate something. Yet the hearer may understand the sentences in which the speaker has been unsuccessful in singling out any object.

What are we to say, then, of the meaning—or sense—of proper names?

We can say that proper names have both meaning and reference—and reference—without thereby saying that they have *attributive* senses, in the sense defined above. (Here we may recall Wittgenstein's remark: 'I use the name "N" without a *fixed* meaning.'[3]) We shall speak of the *demonstrative sense* and of the *secondary sense* of proper names—both to be distinguished from the *attributive sense*.

To locate the demonstrative sense of a proper name, let us look back at our concept of *indirect attribution*. We have said that, when a person indirectly attributes a property to an object, then he singles out the object by means of a certain identifying relation—a relation which is such that the object is *the* thing to which the person bears that relation. The demonstrative sense of proper names is to be explicated by reference to such relations.

If I use a proper name in speaking to you, then the *demonstrative sense* of that name on that occasion will pertain to the relation by means of which I then single out the object—or objects—of the belief I am expressing to you. The identifying relation will be a relation such that the bearer of the name is the thing to which the user of the name bears that relation. On this view, the demonstrative sense of a name is *not* a property of the bearer of the name. It is, rather, a relational property that the user of the name attributes to himself. The property, therefore, is a property of the *user* of the name—provided there is a bearer of the name. And the corresponding relation is one which the user of the name bears only to the bearer of the name.

Let us consider a very simple example. I say to you: 'Tom has been arrested'. I use the name 'Tom' in thus speaking to you, because I assume that you use 'Tom' for the same person as I do. (But if I knew that you called him 'Bill' and that you didn't know that I called him 'Tom', then I might say 'Bill has been arrested'.) In thus speaking to you, I may thereby think of Tom as being the person who lives in the house at which I am looking. The speaker's demonstrative sense of 'Tom' on this occasion might be expressed by me as 'The person who lives in the house at which I'm looking'. If I use 'Tom' in this way, then I attribute to myself the property of being such that there is just one person who lives in the house at which I am looking; or, more exactly, I attribute to myself the property of being a thing which is such that there is just one person who lives in the house at which that thing is looking. But in saying to you: 'Tom has been arrested', I am *not* thereby *telling* you that the person who lives in the house at which 'I'm looking has been arrested. (To tell you the latter might not serve my purpose at all, for perhaps I know that *you* think that someone other than Tom lives in the house at which I'm looking.) On hearing me, you might then take 'Tom' to designate the person from whom you bought your automobile; in such a case, the hearer's meaning of 'Tom' could then be expressed by you as 'the person from whom I bought my automobile'. If my communication is successful, then there will be two relations R and S such that: I attribute to Tom, as the thing that bears R to me, the property of being arrested, and you will attribute to him, as the thing that bears S to you, the property of being arrested; the only *proposition* we both need to accept in this situation is the proposition that someone has been arrested.

There is no reason to suppose, then, that when I use a proper name in successfully communicating with you then I use the name with the same demonstrative sense as you do. And there is no reason to suppose that, on the different occasions when I single out a given object, I always do so in the same way. On one occasion of using a name, I may conceive of one identifying relation I bear to the object and on another occasion I may conceive of quite another. Hence the demonstrative meanings of a proper name—the speaker's demonstrative meaning and the hearer's demonstrative meaning—may vary from one occasion to another. Neither of these meanings is constituted by a sense which is rigidly associated with the name. Perhaps, on one occasion when I use the name 'Aristotle', the speaker's meaning may be conveyed by 'the author of the book I own with *"Metaphysics"* on its title page', and on another occasion it may better be conveyed by 'the author of the book I own with *"Physics"* on its title page'.

It is quite possible, then, that a proper name may lose one meaning and take on another—while continuing to name the same object. And in the case of most of the proper names that are used by any given speaker, it is quite likely that their original meanings have been completely forgotten. Hence the present view of proper names differs in a fundamental way from those contemporary theories which attribute a special significance to occasion of one's *first* use of a proper name.[4]

What I have called the demonstrative sense of a proper name is only a *part* of the speaker's meaning of that name. The other part—which I shall call the *secondary sense* of the name—is suggested by this fact: the speaker, in using the name, means to indicate that his present use is also his ordinary use of that name. The speaker's secondary sense of the name 'Tom' will the following property of the speaker: that of using 'Tom' in the way in which he ordinarily uses it.

Thus, in the case of our example above, I use 'Tom' with the demonstrative sense of being the person who lives in the house at which I am looking. (I use it to attribute to myself the property of looking at just one house and at a house in which just one person lives.) And I use it with the secondary sense of using the name 'Tom' in the way I ordinarily use it. (I mean to attribute indirectly to Tom the property of being such that I usually call him 'Tom'.)

I shall consider below the reasons for supposing that proper names thus have secondary senses. Let us now try to say more precisely how these concepts might be explicated.

The Intentional Explication of Sense and Reference

Proper names, then, do have a meaning on any occasion of their use; this meaning is a function of the demonstrative senses and the secondary senses that they have on such occasions. They may have one meaning for the speaker and another meaning for the hearer and, even if they remain constant in their referential use, they may be used with different meanings on different occasions. Their meanings need not be a part of the *content* that the sentences in which they are used are intended to convey,[5] and the demonstrative sense and the secondary sense of a proper name are not properties of the *bearer* of the name, but properties that the *user* of the name attributes to himself.[6]

I now suggest how the *sense* and the *reference* of proper names may be explicated intentionally. Such an explication would make use of the intentional concept of direct attribution. It would also make use of the causal concept of *expression* and presuppose that a speech act can express an intentional state. That is to say, it presupposes that a speech act can express the properties that the speaker directly attributes to himself.

Consider a person x who indirectly attributes a property G to a thing y. There will be a certain relation R which is such that x attributes the property G to y *as* the thing to which he, x, bears the relation R, and therefore x will have the relational property which consists of his bearing R to exactly one thing.

Suppose now that x performs a speech act which *expresses* his attribution. We assume that, in the first instance, this act expresses the property he directly attributes to himself. We assume, further, that it is in virtue of certain features (parts, aspects) of the speech act that the speaker expresses certain features (parts, aspects) of the attribution. (We need not presuppose that the speech act is a matter of talking or writing, in the ordinary sense of these words, or even that it involves *words*, in the ordinary sense of the word 'word'.)

There will be one feature of the speech act, then, which is such that, in virtue of that feature of the act, the speaker expresses the *content* of his indirect attribution—i.e., he expresses the fact that he is attributing the property G to something. This may be said to be the *predicative* feature of the act. In virtue of another feature of the act he expresses the fact that he bears R to just one thing. This may be said to be the *demonstrative* feature of the act.

The relational property which consists of being such that one bears R to exactly one thing may be said to be the *demonstrative sense* of the demonstrative feature of the act, and the thing to which the speaker bears the relation in question—in this case, y—may be said to be the *designatum* of that feature of the act.

If the speech act is performed in a language such as English, then that part of it which is the uttering of a predicative expression may be the predicative feature of the act, and that part which is the uttering of a proper name or a demonstrative may be the demonstrative feature of the act. We may then say, by a kind of courtesy, that the predicative expression has, as its sense, the sense of the predicative feature of the act, and that the proper name or demonstrative has, as its sense and its designatum, the sense and the designatum (if any) of the demonstrative feature of the act.

The sense and reference of the proper name are therefore a function of the speaker's intentional state—his direct attribution of a property to himself, and this intentional state presupposes neither an 'outer' nor an 'inner' language.

What we have said about speaker's meaning may be applied, *mutatis mutandis*, to hearer's meaning.

The first person pronoun or other devices the speaker may use to indicate himself may be explicated in a similar fashion. When a person expresses the direct attribution of a property to himself, then, in virtue of one feature of that act, he will express the fact that the attribution is a direct one. This feature could be said to be the *self-demonstrative* feature of the act, and the speaker could be said to be the designatum of that feature. And if he expresses that feature of his act by means of the first person pronoun, then we could say—once again, by a kind of courtesy—that the personal pronoun has, for its designatum in this use, the designatum of the self-demonstrative feature of the act.

If a person thus uses a name or a demonstrative, he uses it in a way that *purports to designate* something. We have noted that Quine's intentional expression 'purports to designate' is sometimes convenient. Thus the name 'Satan' may not actually designate anything, but in the uses of many people it is *thought* to designate something—it *purports to designate* something.

We now consider, finally, the concept of a *secondary sense*. If a speaker does in fact use a name in expressing the demonstrative feature of his act, then the secondary sense of that name will be the following property which the speaker attributes to himself:

that of using the name to designate the thing he usually uses it to designate.

This, then, is the way in which linguistic reference might be explicated in terms of thought. I therefore offer these suggestions in support of what I have called the primacy of the intentional.

Names and Reference

To understand what the preceding definitions involve, let us consider a possible example and some of the questions to which it gives rise.[7]

Suppose Sally has invited Charles to dinner. At the appointed hour she hears a knock on the door. But, as luck would have it, the person at the door is not Charles but another friend, Ned, who has not been invited. Sally says: 'Charles is at the door'.

Our definitions, in application to this example, would seem to imply that Sally is using the name 'Charles' to designate Ned. But if this is so, then the following questions arise: (1) If, as we may suppose, Sally is very well acquainted with both Charles and Ned, how could she make the mistake of using 'Charles' to refer to Ned? (2) Sally's statement, 'Charles is at the door', is false. But if she is using 'Charles' to designate Ned, then how could it be false? (3) If she believes that the one who is at the door is the one who has been invited, then, according to the account of indirect attribution that has been proposed, she indirectly attributes to Ned—who has not been invited—the property of being invited. Do the proposed definitions commit us, then, to saying that Sally now believes that Ned has been invited?

The definitions do commit us to saying that, in this situation, Sally has used 'Charles' to designate Ned. And this would have been clear to Ned, for he might well have said: 'Please don't call me "Charles"'. I suggest, then, that the three questions should be answered as follows:

(1) The fact that Sally is very well acquainted both with Charles and with Ned need not prevent her from mistaking one of them for the other, and when she does mistake the one for the other, she will attribute to the one properties that she thinks belong to the other. (2) 'If she is using "Charles" for Ned, how can it be

that her statement, "Charles is at the door", is false?' The statement is false because Ned does not satisfy the seconday sense of the name 'Charles': that is to say, Ned is not the one whom Sally usually calls 'Charles'. (3) 'Did Sally believe that Ned was invited?' That the answer is 'no' will be suggested by still another principle—what I shall call the 'believes that' principle.[8]

We have emphasized that the primary sense of believing is direct attribution, and in Chapter 4 we characterized *de dicto* belief—the acceptance of propositions or states of affairs—as a particular type of direct attribution. It is often assumed that the 'believes that' locution is an indication of *de dicto* belief and that the 'that'-clause expresses the proposition or state of affairs that is accepted. But if what I have been saying is correct, then this assumption is false. Nevertheless, 'She believes that Ned has been invited' may tell us something that we are not told by the sentence: 'She believes, with respect to Ned, that he has been invited'. What could this something be if it is not the acceptance of a certain proposition? The 'believes that' principle tells us what it is.

The principle may be put as follows:

> P1 If it can be correctly said of a person S in English that 'he believes that a is F' (where 'a' occupies the place of a proper name and 'F' the place of a predicative expression), then S has a belief which could be expressed in his language in such a way that its English translation could be paraphrased as 'a is F', wherein the name replacing 'a' is the English version of a certain proper name in S's language.

If this principle is true, as I believe it is, then we cannot say of Sally: 'she *believes that* Ned has been invited'. What we should say is that in this situation, where she has mistaken Ned for Charles, she believes *with respect to* Ned that he has been invited.

I have used the word 'correctly' in my statement of the 'believes that' locution. Unfortunately, we *do* on occasion use the 'believe that' locution when the above principle is not satisfied, and therefore in a way that I would say is incorrect. Thus I may say: 'The prowler believes that Charles has called the police' even though I am quite sure that the prowler has no name for Charles. In such a case, it seems to me, the 'believes that' locution is being used incorrectly. Had I wanted to speak more philosophically, I would have said: 'The prowler believes, with respect to Charles, that he is in there'. (Descriptive phrases may also occur in such incorrect uses. Compare: 'His comrades at school thought that the future Pope would never be a clergyman', and: 'Columbus believed that the land we call "Cuba" is in the Indian Ocean'.)

Mention in Use

Let us now return to the concept of a *secondary sense*. The secondary sense of a name on any occasion, I have said, is the property the speaker then attributes to himself of using that name in the way that he ordinarily uses it. So, if I use the name 'Tom', I mean to be saying something about 'Tom' as well as about Tom. Is it really plausible to suppose that we ordinarily thus talk *about* the proper names that we use? I think that it is.

Doubtless proper names are often used, 'in *suppositio materialis*', as names for themselves, as in 'Boston is a noun'. It also seems clear that, as Anton Marty put it, a name may be thought of as abbreviating 'the thing that has this name'.[9] In such cases the name is taken in an obviously secondary sense. Thus, if one says: 'There are at least two Portlands in the United States', what one wishes to convey is that there are at least two cities in the United States have the name 'Portland'. Again, if the teacher says to his students: 'William E. Borah was a United States Senator', then it is very likely that his message could also be put by saying: 'There was once a United States Senator named "William E. Borah".'

The fact that names are used in this secondary sense, of 'the thing that has this name', has also led to philosophical puzzlement. For example, what are we saying when we put the 'is' of identity between proper names, as in 'Cicero is Tully?' (What does one *learn* when one is first told: 'Cicero was identical with Tully'?) Here it is likely that we are using the names in their secondary sense to say something about the names. We are not saying, of course, that the names are identical; we are saying, rather, that the thing that has the one name is identical with the thing that has the other. 'The thing designated by "Cicero" in our language is identical with the thing designated by "Tully" in our language'. Or, better, 'The name "Cicero" is such that the thing it designates in our language and in our culture circle is identical with the thing designated by "Tully" in our language and in our culture circle'.

According to what I have said, if we are justified in using proper names in reporting other people's beliefs (as in 'Jones believed that Cicero was identical with Tully'), then the beliefs in question are in part beliefs *about* those names. If I say, pointing to you, 'He says that Charles is dishonest', I am likely to be saying these two things: (a) that you use your word for Charles in order to express your indirect attribution to Charles of the property of being dishonest; and (b) that you believe, with respect to the name you usually use to designate Charles, that the person it designates is dishonest.

The 'believes that' principle may also suggest a solution to a puzzle set forth and discussed by Saul Kripke.[10] Kripke envisages a Frenchman, Pierre, who once sincerely expressed himself by saying: '*Londres est joli.*' Subsequently Pierre is taken to England, not knowing that London is the city he designates in his native language by the name '*Londres*'. He learns English, visits an ugly part of London, and says, again sincerely, 'London is not pretty'. He has not changed his mind about London, for he would still sincerely say: '*Londres est joli*', if he were speaking with a Frenchman, and he has not made any errors in English. Yet we now seem able to convict him of contradicting himself. On the basis of his French statement we would conclude

Pierre believes that London is pretty.

And on the basis of his English statement we would conclude

Pierre believes that London is not pretty.

And so we seem to be attributing contradictory beliefs to Pierre. How can this be?

One may be tempted to solve the puzzle by saying that Pierre merely had different *de re* beliefs about London. One would then replace our two statements, above, by 'Pierre believes, with respect to London, that it is pretty' and 'Pierre believes, with respect to London, that it is not pretty'. Two such *de re* beliefs, we know, are no indication of contradiction or logical ineptitude; for a person may not *know* that the thing to which he attributes the one property is identical with the thing to which he attributes the negation of that property. But this course is not available to us. The fact that Pierre used the proper names 'Londres' and 'London' in the expression of his beliefs indicates that such a *de re* formulation leaves something out. What, then, does it leave out?

We would be committing the proper name fallacy if we were to say, on the basis of our data, 'The proposition that London is pretty was accepted by Pierre, and the proposition that London is not pretty was accepted by Pierre'. For it is problematic whether the sentences *'Londres est joli'* and 'London is pretty' express propositions.

Let us view the matter, then, in terms of the 'believes that' principle. If we interpret the two sentences: 'Pierre believes that London is pretty' and 'Pierre believes that London is not pretty' in accordance with this principle, it will be obvious that they do not attribute contradictory beliefs to Pierre. The first sentence is true in virtue of the fact that Pierre attributes to himself the property of being such that the thing he usually uses *'Londres'* to designate is pretty. And the second sentence is true in virtue of the fact that he attributes to himself the property of being such that the thing he usually uses 'London' to designate is a thing that is not pretty.

The fact that the 'believe that' principle thus seems to solve the puzzle in question and that other plausible solutions do not seem to be at hand may be taken as a kind of confirmation of the principle.

Negative Existentials

If the primary function of proper names is that of indicating the object of an indirect attribution, how are we to understand their role in such negative existentials as 'Tom does not exist' and 'Moses did not exist'? One is not saying of the object of attribution that that object does not exist or did not exist.[11]

It was clear to Wittgenstein that names are inconstant in their meanings, and he refers to this fact in dealing with the problem of negative existentials. In considering the sentence 'Moses did not exist', he mentions various definite descriptions that one might substitute for the proper name 'Moses' (for example, 'the man who led the Israelites through the wilderness' and 'the man who as a child was taken out of the Nile by Pharaoh's daughter') and he then observes: 'But when I make a statement about Moses—am I always ready to substitute some *one* of these descriptions for "Moses"? I shall perhaps say: By "Moses" I understand the man who did what the Bible relates of Moses, or at any rate a good deal of it. But how much? Have I decided how much must be proved false for me to give up my proposition as false? Has the name "Moses" got a fixed and unequivocal use for me in all possible cases?—Is it not the case that I have, so to speak, a whole series of props in readiness, and am ready to lean on one if another should be taken from under me and vice versa?'[12] Wittgenstein then goes on to suggest that, if we are to understand the use of the negative statement, 'Moses did not exist', we should not assume that it presupposes some fixed sense of the proper name 'Moses'.

What are we to say more positively about such negative statements? Suppose, for example, that I were to say to you: 'Tom does not exist—and never did'. What would I be trying to tell you?

It would be a mistake to suppose that there is a certain *proposition* which such a sentence is intended to express. Hence we are not looking for the *analysis* of such a proposition. We are asking: What kind of an attribution is expressed when I say to you 'Tom does not exist—and never did?'

There are various possibilities.

I might be telling you that the relational identifying properties by means of which *you* think you can single out one thing and a thing you call 'Tom' do not single out anything—they have no correlates. In such a case, the object of my indirect attribution would be you. I would be saying that you do not have the properties in question.

I need not, however, thus be speaking of you when I say to you 'Tom does not exist'. Possibly the context of utterance presupposes some third person who is the object of indirect attribution. I might be considering the relational identifying properties that *he* attributes to himself and by means of which he thinks he can single out one and only one person and one whom he calls 'Tom'; and I might be saying that these properties have no correlate and hence that they are properties he doesn't have. (This is how we should interpret such a statement as 'The God they worship does not exist.')

Or I might simply be talking about myself: 'The properties *I* thought enabled me to single out one thing and a thing that I called "Tom" don't point to anything—they have no correlate' ... and so on. ('But if Tom never existed, how could you have called him "Tom"?' The answer is that I *thought* I called him 'Tom'—or, more accurately, that I attributed to myself a property of this sort: I thought that there was one and only one thing related to me in such and such a way and that I used 'Tom' to designate that thing. Hence I used the name in a way that merely purports to designate.)

Other negative existentials are to be interpreted analogously. The names which are thus used in connection with the denial of existence do not have their ordinary speaker's meaning or hearer's meaning. What sort of meaning do they have? It would seem clear that their meaning is a variant of what I have called their secondary sense.

We should note, finally, that 'Tom *might not* have existed' is *not* analogous to 'Tom did not exist'. For the former statement expresses an attribution that is intended to have Tom as its object, but the latter does not.[13]

The Problem of Mistaken Indication

Consider the following objection: 'What if, on a certain occasion, someone says: "Aristotle discovered the principles of the syllogism", but uses the proper name "Aristotle" with a meaning, or demonstrative sense, that does not connect up with him? Perhaps the person is thinking of Aristotle as the author of a certain passage; but in fact the passage was inserted into the Aristotelian corpus by a later follower. Your theory implies that, in such a case, the person will not have succeeded in designating Aristotle—and that he will be referring to the other person instead. But surely this is wrong. The person's statement—'Aristotle discovered the principles of the syllogism'—is nevertheless *true* and the person *is* telling us, with respect to Aristotle, that he discovered the syllogism.

The theory does imply that, in the situation imagined, the *speaker* will not have singled out Aristotle for himself. That is to say, the speaker's meaning of the words that he utters will involve a relation that singles out someone other than Aristotle for the speaker. It will not follow from this that the *hearer's* meaning does not involve a relation that singles out Aristotle for the hearer. If the hearer *has* successfully singled out Aristotle, by means of some identifying relation that Aristotle bears to *him*, then we may say that the *hearer's* meaning of 'Aristotle' does single out Aristotle. The fact that the speaker's meaning is defective, then, will not prevent the hearer from understanding the content that the speaker wished to convey, and it will not prevent the speaker himself from singling out Aristotle and connecting the statement with other things he has said or believes about Aristotle.

Multiple Objects

The primary use of proper names, we have said, is that of indicating or demonstrating the object of indirect attribution. What, then, of those sentences in which we make use of a number of proper names?

An indirect attribution may have a multiplicity of objects. Consider, for example, what is expressed by the relatively simple sentence, 'John loves Mary'. One may be tempted to say that the sentence expresses an indirect attribution which has as its object John and which has as its content the property of loving Mary. But I would say that, given an adequate theory of properties, it is problematic whether there *is* a property corresponding to the expression 'loves Mary'. If the proper name 'Mary' had a fixed attributive sense, then perhaps we could say that the speaker was attributing to John the property of loving the thing that exemplifies that sense, but if the name has no sense, then this interpretation is not available to us.

And, in fact, the statement 'John loves Mary' is more plausibly interpreted in another way. If, for the moment, we think of an assertion as a recommendation to believe, then we could interpret 'John loves Mary' as expressing this recommendation to believe: 'Consider any relation R by means of which you single out Mary: attribute to yourself the property of being such that the thing to which you bear R loves the thing to which you bear S'. I would say then that in one of its ordinary uses, the statement 'John loves Mary' expresses this fact: there is a relation R such that the speaker believes himself to bear R just to John, there is a relation S such that the speaker believes himself to bear S just to Mary, and he directly attributes to himself the property of being such that the thing to which he bears R loves the thing to which he bears S.

Statements containing a greater number of proper names may be interpreted analogously. We shall consider further complications in the final chapter.

A Note on Rigid Designators

One important distinction between proper names and definite descriptions is suggested by Kripke's thesis that proper names are 'rigid designators' and definite descriptions are not. He puts this distinction as follows: 'Let's call something a *rigid designator* if in any possible world it designates the same object, a *non-rigid* or *accidental designator* if that is not the case'.[14] The distinction is thus formulated by reference to Kripke's ontology of possible worlds—where possible worlds are viewed as particular things, indefinitely many of which are such that the particular individuals of the actual world can be said to be *in* them. Given what we shall say in the *Appendix* about ontology and about worlds, there is no reason to believe that there *are* the possible entities to which Kripke thus appeals. Or, more accurately, there is no reason to suppose that there are possible individuals which are worlds and that some of these individuals are capable of containing the individuals that are to be found in this world. But Kripke's distinction between rigid and non-rigid designators need not presuppose such an ontology. Let us try to locate the facts in virtue of which names—but not ordinary definite descriptions—are those said to be 'rigid designators'.

We may illustrate what is behind the distinction by contrasting the proper name 'Jimmy Carter' and the definite description 'The President of the United States in 1979' (which description we shall abbreviate in what immediately follows as 'the President').

One may use 'the President' in English in such a way that in that use it does not designate Mr Carter. Here are five examples: (1) 'Had Gerald Ford won the 1974 election, then he would be the President'; (2) 'Governor Reagan hopes that he will be the President'; (3) 'His illness prevented Hubert Humphrey from being the President'; (4) 'It was possible for a woman to be the President'; and (5) 'It was the duty of every American citizen to help select the person who would be the President'. The first example is a case of a counterfactual; the second is intentional; the third is causal; the fourth is modal; and the fifth is ethical.

Each of these uses of 'the President' illustrates the 'non-rigid' character of definite descriptions. What is common to the five examples?

The descriptive phrase, 'the President', is not subject to existential generalization in any of these sentences. That is to say, we may not replace 'the President' in any of these sentences by a free variable and then bind that variable by an existential quantifier. For example, 'Governor Reagan wanted to be the President' does not warrant the inference to 'There exists an x such that Governor Reagan wanted to be x.'

Let us say that a singular term is *used non-designatively* in a sentence if it occurs in that sentence and if neither the sentence nor its negation is thus susceptible to existential generalization over the singular term. The thesis that proper names are rigid designators may now be put by saying that proper names are singular terms which cannot be used non-designatively.

May we say, of definite descriptions, that any such expression *can* thus be used non-designatively? The statement would not be true of 'the person identical with Jimmy Carter' or 'the tallest man in Boston'. But perhaps we can qualify our thesis by saying: Any definite description, not containing a proper part that is used as a demonstrative or proper name, can be used non-designatively.

What if we said: 'Senator Baker would just be another Jimmy Carter'? Are we here using 'Jimmy Carter' in such a way that it designates Jimmy Carter? I would say that the answer is yes. For what we would be saying, in essence, is that Senator Baker has many of those characteristics that typify Jimmy Carter. Frege had noted that a proper name may sometimes be used as what he called a 'concept-word'; his example was 'Trieste is no Vienna'.[15] But doesn't 'Trieste is no Vienna' tell us that we must not expect to find in Trieste the sort of thing that is typical of Vienna? The name 'Vienna', in the latter sentence, functions as a name and *not* as a concept-word.

Notes

1   See Alvin Plantinga, 'De Essentia', in *Grazer Philosophische Studien*, Vol. VII (1979).
2   Compare the distinction between the 'referential' and the 'attributive' uses of definite descriptions in Keith Donnellan, 'Reference and Definite Descriptions', in H. Feigl, W. Sellars and K. Lehrer, eds., *New Readings in Philosophical Analysis* (New York: Appleton-Century-Crofts, 1972), pp. 59–71; the paper first appeared in 1972.
3   Ludwig Wittgenstein, *Philosophical Investigations* (Oxford: Basil Blackwell, 1953), p. 37e. Compare John R. Searle's remark about 'the poverty of a rigid sense-reference, denotation-connotation approach to problems of the theory of meaning'; quoted from 'Proper Names', *Mind*, LXVII (1958), pp. 166–73 (the quotation is from p. 172). Compare also Donnellan's, 'Proper Names and Identifying Descriptions', in D. Davidson and G. Harman, eds., *Semantics of Natural Languages* (Dordrecht: D. Reidel, 1972), pp. 356–79.
4   Compare David Kaplan, 'Quantifying In', *Synthese*, XIX (1968–69), pp. 178–214; and Diana Ackerman, 'Proper Names, Propositional Attitudes and Non-Descriptive Connotations', *Philosophical Studies*, XXXV (1979), pp. 55–69.
5   This point has been suggested—but I believe not fully endorsed—by Saul Kripke. Using his terminology, we could say that the primary function of a proper name is that of a 'reference fixer'. See his 'Naming and Necessity', in Gilbert Harman and Donald Davidson, eds., *Semantics of Natural Language* (Dordrecht: D. Reidel, 1972), pp. 763–9; see especially p. 277. But Kripke seems to emphasize the importance of the occasion of one's first use of the proper name.
6   This general conception of proper names (with the exception of the doctrine of secondary senses) is similar in fundamental respects to a theory set forth by Arthur W. Burks in 1951; see his 'A Theory of Proper Names', *Philosophical Studies*, II (1951), pp. 31–4. Burke holds that proper names are 'synonymous with indexical definite descriptions', rejects the view that they have identifying properties as their senses, and notes that their meaning may vary from one use to another. But where I have defined the use of 'this' in terms of the use of the first person, and have explicated the latter by reference to direct attribution, Burks takes 'this' as his basic demonstrative or indexical.
7   The example and the questions were suggested to me by Lynne Baker.
8   This principle is what Kripke calls a 'disquotational principle'. See his 'A Puzzle about Belief', in Avishai Margalit, ed., *Meaning and Use* (Dordrecht: D. Reidel Publishing Company, 1976), pp. 239–88; see especially p. 248. Kripke also formulates such a principle, but one presupposing that sentences containing proper names are used to express propositions.
9   Marty said that the name is taken 'in der Bedeutung des *mit diesem Namen Genannten*'. See Anton Marty, *Untersuchungen zur Grundlegung der allgemeinen Grammatik und Sprachphilosophie* (Halle: Max Niemeyer, 1908), p. 509.
10   See Kripke's 'A Puzzle about Belief'.
11   For a general statement of the problem of negative existentials, see Richard L. Cartwright, 'Negative Existentials', *Journal of Philosophy*, LVII (1960), pp. 629–39.
12   Wittgenstein, *op. cit.*, p. 37e.
13   What of proper names in fiction—as in 'Dr Jekyll was a physician'? I would accept the answer which, I understand, has been given by Kripke: namely, that

when the story-teller says such things, he is not *using* the proper name, but is only *pretending* to use it.

14 Saul Kripke, 'Naming and Necessity', in G. Harman and D. Davidson, eds., *Semantics of Natural Language* (Dordrecht: D. Reidel, 1972), pp. 253–355; the quotation is on pp. 269–70.

15 G. Frege, *Translations from the Philosophical Writings of Gottlob Frege*, ed. P. Geach and M. Black (Oxford: Basil Blackwell, 1952), p. 50.

Chapter 7
CERTAINTY AND THE UNITY OF CONSCIOUSNESS

Introduction

ALL my beliefs, in the final analysis, are direct attributions. I am the *object* of these attributions, but no part of their *content*. The content of any such attribution is the property I thereby attribute to myself.

If I directly attribute the property of standing to myself, then, I may be said to believe myself to be standing. And even though there are no 'I'-propositions, I may express my belief by saying 'I believe that I am standing'. If my direct attribution is also evident to me, then it will be evident to me that I am standing. And if it is also the case that I *am* standing, then I will know that I am standing.

The *object* of such knowledge, like that of direct attribution, will be the subject himself, and the *content* of the knowledge will be the property he directly attributes to himself.

If the content I thus attribute to myself were to include my individual essence, then perhaps we could say—somewhat loosely—that there is a sense in which I am a part of the *content* of my direct attributions, but, we have said, there is no good reason for believing that my individual essence is included in any of the things I attribute to myself.

What, then, of the traditional doctrine according to which I can be certain that I exist? One way of putting this doctrine is to say that, for each person, there is a set of first-person propositions each of which is empirically certain and directly evident for that person. But if there are no 'I'-propositions, we cannot accept this version of the traditional doctrine. And, one may wonder, if I am no part of the content of that which is empirically certain and directly evident, then how can I be certain of my own existence? 'The given', it would seem, must be 'subjectless'.

It may be implausible to say: 'He is certain of his own existence' if we take this to mean that the direct attribution of existence is certain for him, for it is problematic whether existence is an attribute or property. But we *can* say: 'He is certain that he exists' if we take it to mean that there is a property such that the direct attribution of that property is certain for him.

To understand the nature of this empirical certainty, we must consider the general nature of such epistemic concepts.

Some Epistemic Concepts

The simplest way of setting forth the vocabulary of the theory of evidence, or epistemology, is to take as undefined the locution, '—is more reasonable than . . . for S at t' (or, alternatively, '—is epistemically preferable to . . . for S at t'). Epistemic reasonability could be understood in terms of the general requirement to try to have a set of logically independent beliefs which is such that the true beliefs outnumber the false beliefs by as large a number as possible. The principles of epistemic preferability are the principles one should follow if one is to fulfil this requirement. (It should be noted that the requirement is so formulated that the requirement to have true beliefs receives greater emphasis than the requirement not to have false beliefs.)

The epistemic locution we have taken as undefined is obviously applicable to propositional acceptance, or *de dicto* belief, where we can say that accepting one proposition is more or less reasonable than accepting another, but its application can readily be extended to direct attribution.

In order to characterize the relevant epistemic concepts in their application to such attribution, we shall introduce the concept of *withholding* the attribution of a property. Consider a person and a property such that (a) the person does *not* directly attribute that property to himself and (b) he does not directly attribute the *negation* of that property to himself: such a person may be said to *withhold* the direct attribution of that property.

Among the general principles of epistemic preferability is the fact that such preferability is transitive and asymmetric. If one attribution, or withholding, is more reasonable for a given subject at a given time than a second, and if the second is more reasonable than a third, then the first is more reasonable than the third. And if one is more reasonable than another, then the other is not more reasonable than the one.

We may also affirm the following principle: If, for a certain subject at a certain time, withholding the direct attribution of a given property is *not* more reasonable than the direct attribution of that property, then the direct attribution of that property *is* more reasonable than the direct attribution of the negation of that property. This principle has its analogue in the following *de dicto* epistemic principle: if withholding a proposition is *not* more reasonable than accepting it, then accepting it is more reasonable than accepting its negation. 'If agnosticism is not more reasonable than theism, then theism is more reasonable than atheism'.[1]

Given these principles and others, we may formulate definitions of a variety of fundamental epistemic concepts. We could say, for example, that the direct attribution of a given property is epistemically *unacceptable* for a given subject at a given time, provided only that withholding that property is more reasonable for that subject at that time than directly attributing it. In saying that the attitude is 'unacceptable', I do not mean that the believer *finds* it unacceptable. I mean something more objective—something that could also be put by saying that the attitude ought not to be taken, or that it is an attitude that it would be unreasonable to take. We could say that an attribution is *counterbalanced* if and only if the direct attribution of that property is no more nor less reasonable than is the direct attribution of the negation of that property. One might say that there is nothing which it is more reasonable to withhold than that which is counterbalanced.

We may also distinguish several different epistemic levels that the direct attribution of a property may occupy for a given subject at a given time. Thus we have:

Having some presumption in its favour;

Acceptability;

Being beyond reasonable doubt;

Being evident;

Being certain.

Each of these conepts may be said to provide a sense for the expression 'epistemically justified'—certainty constituting the highest degree of epistemic justification and having some presumption in its favour the lowest.

A direct attribution of a property could be said to *have some presumption in its favour*, provided only that the direct attribution of that property is more reasonable than the direct attribution of its negation. A direct attribution of a property is *acceptable* if it is not unacceptable. And a direct attribution of a property could be said to be *beyond reasonable doubt*—or, simply, *reasonable*—provided only that the direct attribution of that property is more reasonable than withholding that property.

Ascending to still higher epistemic levels, we may now consider *the evident*—where the evident is thought of as that which distinguishes knowledge from true belief that isn't knowledge. This epistemic category would seem to fall between that which is beyond reasonable doubt, on the one hand, and that which is objectively certain, on the other. It is beyond reasonable doubt for me that the roof on this building will continue to be here tomorrow. But this fact is not now *evident*, and will not be evident before tomorrow. And tomorrow, when it *is* evident, it will not be objectively *certain* for me, in the sense in which we will explicate the latter concept. How, then, are we to characterize the evident?

An attribution may be said to be *evident*, for a given person at a given time, provided, first, that the attribution is then beyond reasonable doubt for that person, and provided, secondly, that it is one of those attributions upon which it is reasonable for him to base his assignments of probability. Probability, as Bishop Butler said, is or ought to be 'the guide of life'.[2] When the reasonable man makes a practical decision, he will base his decision, in part, upon certain probabilities. These will be probabilities which are probabilities relative to certain premisses—namely, to premisses that are *evident*. An *evident* attribution, then, is by definition an attribution which it is thus reasonable to use as a premiss; in other words, it is such that thus using it as a premiss is more reasonable than not thus using it as a premiss.

Perhaps this account of the evident may be illustrated by reference to our example about the roof. If I were making certain probability calculations about roofs, say, in order to decide what type of roof to construct upon what type of house, then I could use as a premiss the fact that this roof is on this house today. But

I should not *now* take as a premiss the fact this roof will be on this house tomorrow—despite the fact that such a premiss is now beyond reasonable doubt for me.

Finally, there is the concept of objective certainty. The direct attribution of a property may be said to be objectively *certain* for a person provided that these conditions hold: that the direct attribution of that property is beyond reasonable doubt for that person; and that it is at least as reasonable for him as is the direct attribution of any other property. If the attribution of the property of being F is thus certain for a subject, then he may be said to be certain that *he* is F.

These epistemic expressions may be read in another way. For example, if we may say, of the property of being F, that the direct attribution of that property is beyond reasonable doubt for a certain subject x, then we may also say: 'It is beyond reasonable doubt for x that *he* is F', and analogously for the other epistemic concepts just defined.

We must take care not to be misled by syntax at this point. The propositional locution, 'It is beyond reasonable doubt for x that *he* is F', may tempt one to suppose that there is a certain proposition corresponding to the expression 'he is F' and that this proposition is one which is beyond reasonable doubt for the subject x. But 'It is beyond reasonable for x that he is F' does not imply that there is a proposition corresponding to the expression 'he is F'. In this respect it may be compared with the locution 'He believes himself to be F'. The later tells us only that he has directly attributed the property of being F to himself; and the former tells us only that, for him, directly attributing that property is more reasonable than withholding it.

The epistemic concepts which thus apply to direct attributions have their analogues, which may be applied to propositions.

The Self-Presenting

There are certain properties—many, if not all, of them psychological or 'Cartesian'—which may be said to *present themselves* to the subject who has them. One example is feeling sad; another is thinking about a golden mountain; another is believing oneself to be wise; and still another may be suggested by the awkward locution 'is appeared redly to'.

A property P may be called *self-presenting* provided only that P is necessarily such that (a) nothing that has it directly attributes to itself the negation of P; (b) every property it entails is necessarily such that everything that can have it can also consider its having it; and (c) if P entails the capacity to have a certain property, then P entails that property.

A property P is said to *entail* a property Q, provided only these conditions hold: P is necessarily such that, if something has it, then something has Q, and whatever conceives it conceives Q.

Condition (b) in our formulation has the effect of restricting self-presenting properties to individual things. Hence no property capable of being universal (e.g., the property of being such that there are stones) will be self-presenting.

We will assume that every self-presenting property is necessarily such that, if an individual has it, if he considers his having it (that is, if he thinks of himself as having it), then, *ipso facto*, he will directly attribute it to himself.

We could distinguish the 'self-presenting' from the 'self-presented'. A property that is self-presenting may not be considered and therefore it will not be *self-presented*.[3] But, if it is considered by the subject who has it, then he will accept the fact that he has it and the property may be said, therefore, to be self-presented.

We may say that *all* self-presenting properties are psychological or 'Cartesian'. Indeed, we could define *consciousness* by reference to the self-presenting. Thus we could say that a thing is conscious if and only if it has a self-presenting property. This concept of consciousness would seem to be the same as Descartes' concept of *thinking*:

By the word thought I understand all that of which we are conscious as operating in us. And that is why not alone understanding, willing, imagining, but also feeling, are here the same thing as thought . . . If I mean to talk only of my sensation, or my consciously seeming to see or to walk, . . . my assertion now refers only to my mind, which alone is concerned with my feeling or thinking that I see and I walk.[4]

We should note something which may not be clear in the passage from Descartes: that there are *ways of being appeared to*—ways of *sensing*—which are such that being appeared to in those ways is self-presenting. Thus there is what we might call 'a way of being appeared to' which is such that, if you are appeared to in that way, and if you consider your being appeared to in that way, then you will attribute to yourself the property of being appeared to in that way. We shall return to such ways of being appeared to in the following chapter.

I have defined 'self-presenting property' in terms of direct attribution and necessity. And I have said that every self-presenting property is a property which is such that, if while having it, you *consider* your having it, then you will *believe* yourself to have it. (So, perhaps, we should not pride ourselves on being able to define consciousness in terms of self-presentation.)

Let us now note that considering and believing are themselves self-presenting. If you are sad and consider your being sad, then you will attribute sadness to yourself. If you consider your being sad and then consider your considering being sad, then you will believe yourself to consider your being sad. And if you believe yourself to be sad and consider your believing yourself to be sad, then you will believe yourself to believe yourself to be sad.

There is no regress here. We are not saying that if you consider your being sad, then you will believe that you are considering your being sad, And we are not saying that if you believe yourself to be sad, then you will believe yourself to believe yourself to be sad, for we can consider and believe without considering our considering and believing.

Our definition of the self-presenting may be interpreted as telling us that the presence of a self-presenting property is 'indubitable'. This interpretation is correct if 'doubt' is taken to imply conscious withholding of belief. Necessarily, if you have such a property and if you consider your having it, then you will believe yourself to have it; and it you believe yourself to have it, then you cannot at the same time doubt whether you have it. But this type of indubitability should be distinguished from the epistemic concept of *certainty*.

Self-Presentation and Certainty

We have said that the direct attribution of a property is objectively *certain* for a person provided these conditions hold: the direct attribution of that property is beyond reasonable doubt for that person; and it is at least as reasonable for him as is the direct attribution of any other property. Let us now consider the relation of such certainty to that which is self-presenting.

It will be noted that I have not *defined* self-presenting properties by reference to certainty. But if we think of certainty as constituting the highest degree of epistemic justification, then we may say that a person's self-presenting properties *are* objects of certainty for that person.

Indeed we may affirm the following 'material epistemic principle' pertaining to such certainty:

> EP1 If the property of being F is self-presenting, then for every x, if (i) x has the property of being F, and if (ii) x considers his being F, then it is certain for x that he then has the property of being F.

If, as I have said, being sad is a self-presenting property, then, if you are sad and if you consider the question of whether you are sad, it will be certain for you that you are sad. And if considering is also self-presenting, and if you consider your considering whether you are sad, then it will be certain for you that you are considering whether you are sad.

Every self-presenting property provides us with an instance of EP1. Thus we could say:

> For every x, if (i) x has the property of being sad, and if (ii) x considers his being sad, then it is certain for x that he then has the property of being sad.

Our principle illustrates what some have called the *supervenient* character of epistemic justification; for it tells us how positive epistemic status 'is supervenient on a set of non-epistemic facts'.[5] Other material epistemic principles which I shall formulate also illustrate such supervenience. (We could say that a normative property G 'supervenes upon' a non-normative property H, provided only: H is necessarily such that whatever has it has G, but not necessarily such that whoever attributes it attributes G. A 'normative' property—for present purposes—could be said to be any property definable in terms of preferability.) Thus the instance of EP1 cited above tells us that being certain that one is sad supervenes upon the property of being both sad and such that one considers one's being sad.

Principle EP1 pertains to what we might call 'non-propositional certainty'. But we may affirm as a corollary the following principle about propositional certainty: For every x, if it is certain for x that he has the property of being F, then the *proposition* that something is F is one that is empirically certain for x.

The empirical certainty that may thus be yielded by those of our properties that are self-presenting could be said to constitute that which is *directly evident*—or, more exactly, that which is *directly evident a posteriori*. When we have such properties, then our direct attributions of them are directly evident. So, too, for the attribution of those properties which are *entailed* by the self-presenting. (We have said that one property 'entails' another if it is necessarily such that whoever conceives it conceives the other.) And the propositions that are entailed by such attributions may also be said to be directly evident.

The A Priori

The *a posteriori* certainty of that which is self-presenting is to be contrasted with the *a priori* certainty of that which is axiomatic.

In one of its traditional senses, the word 'axiom' is used to refer to a state of affairs which is necessarily such that, if one understands it, then one *sees* that it is true. But let us single out a concept of *axiom* which is analogous to that of the *self-presenting* and which, therefore, we may characterize without the use of epistemic expressions.

It would be in the spirit of the traditional conception to say that an *axiom* is a proposition which is necessarily such that (i) it is true and (ii) whoever considers it accepts it. An axiom, so conceived, has two marks: one the modal property of necessity, and the other the intentional property of being such that it cannot be considered or entertained without being accepted. The *consideration* of a proposition or state of affairs should be distinguished, of course, from the consideration of a *sentence* which happens to express that proposition or state of affairs. Consideration of a proposition or state of affairs involves the conception of an eternal object.

The concept of an axiom, thus defined, is an absolute concept, holding necessarily of certain propositions or states of affairs. What is thus an axiom may or may not be axiomatic *for* a particular individual. To be axiomatic for a particular individual, the axiom must be considered—and therefore also accepted—

by that individual. In other words, a proposition is *axiomatic* for a person provided only that the proposition is an axiom and that the person does consider it. Whatever is thus axiomatic for a person may be said to be *directly evident a priori* for that person.

Can we now formulate a general epistemic principle pertaining to that which is axiomatic? Since our primary concern in the present book is with empirical knowledge and belief, we shall put the present principle in summary form:

> EP2 For every x, and every proposition h, if x can construct a derivation of h which is such that all the premisses of that derivation are axiomatic for x, and each step in the derivation follows axiomatically either from those that precede it or from the premisses, then h is evident for x.

(One proposition may be said to 'follow axiomatically' from another for a person x, provided it is axiomatic for x that if the first is true then the second is true.)

Any axiomatic state of affairs which is thus evident can be said to be something that is known *a priori*. Our principle thus assures us that the sphere of that which is *a priori* may be wider than the sphere of that which is directly evident *a priori*.

Our second epistemic principle is like the first in that the consequent but not the antecedent contains an epistemic term. We have said that the antecedent of the first principle, EP1, is such that the subject can know by reflection whether or not it obtains. Can I know by reflection that a given state of affairs is axiomatic for me?

Mere reflection may not be enough. But if a proposition h is axiomatic for me, then I can know *a priori* that h is thus axiomatic for me. And since I can know directly and immediately *what* it is that I am considering, I can know that the proposition is axiomatic for me.

The knowledge that a property is self-presenting is comparable to the knowledge that a proposition is axiomatic. Thus application of our more general principle EP1 presupposes that we can know *which* properties are self-presenting. Indeed, I would say that it presupposes this general principle about the 'faculty of knowing':

> EP3 For every x and every y, if y is a property and x conceives y, then: it is evident to x that y is self-presenting, if, and only if, y is self-presenting.

The knowledge that a certain property is self-presenting could thus be said to be *a priori*. Like other *a priori* knowledge, however, it presupposes the empirical fact that the knower has conceived certain properties.

The 'I Think'

We turn now to the unity of consciousness.

We begin by considering two things that Kant tells us about it. In setting forth the data for his theory about the synthetic unity of apperception, he makes a positive point and a negative point.

Kant says, positively: 'It must be possible for the "I think" to accompany all my representations, for otherwise something would be represented in me which could not be thought at all, and that is equivalent to saying that the representation would be impossible or at least would be nothing to me'.[6] According to this positive point, then, it is *possible* for the 'I think' to be attached to any object of consciousness. How, then, are we to interpret this metaphor of 'attached to'?

I suggest that, when Kant speaks of 'attaching the "I think"' to a representation, he is speaking of what happens when one directly attributes to himself a self-presenting property. In other words, to say that the subject attaches 'I think' to one of his properties is to say this: the subject has the property; the property is necessarily such that, if one has it and if one considers *whether* one has it, then one will believe oneself to have it; and the subject believes himself to have it.

What I have just said tells us the conditions under which a person may 'attach the "I think"' to his self-presenting states. It does not imply that the subject attaches the 'I think' to *all* his self-presenting states. It tells us only the sense in which, as Kant says, the subject *could* attach the 'I think' to any of these states. The subject need only ask himself, with respect to a certain property that is self-presenting to him, whether he has that property.

And what of Kant's negative point? He says: 'It is obvious that in attaching "I" to our thoughts we designate the subject of inherence only transcendentally, without noting in it any quality whatsoever—in fact without knowing anything of it either by direct acquaintance or otherwise'.[7]

Kant's negative point, I suggest, can be understood by

reference to what we have said about 'I'-propositions and direct attribution. Direct attribution—something that we would normally express in first-person sentences—is *not* a matter of accepting first-person propositions; it is a matter of directly attributing a property to oneself. But the self is the *object* of such attribution and it is not a part of the *content* of such attribution. Kant puts the latter point by saying that we refer to the object of attribution 'without noting in it any quality whatsoever'. The point is reflected in what we have said about the first-person pronoun: it is the only singular term that has no speaker's meaning.

The Concept of a Self

'If a person can consider his attributing sadness to himself, then he has a concept, not only of sadness, but also of *himself*. And if he has a concept of himself, then he must have acquired it by means of an intuition—a type of direct acquaintance. But you have said nothing about such acquaintance.'

The reply is: (a) in considering his attribution of sadness to himself, the person makes use of a concept of *a* self, but not of a concept of *himself*; and (b) he acquires the concept of *a* self in precisely the same way that he acquires the concept of sadness. Let us consider the two points in turn.

The relation expressed by 'He considers his being sad' is analogous to that expressed by 'He believes himself to be sad'. We have spelled out 'He believes himself to be sad' by saying: 'He is an x such that x directly attributes to x the property of being sad'. And we have spelled out 'He considers his being sad'—somewhat awkwardly, to be sure—as 'He is an x such that x directly thinks of x as being sad'. (We have introduced 'directly' so that we may distinguish a concept of indirect consideration analogous to indirect attribution. I can also consider *your* being sad.) One may construe considering as a kind of quasi-attribution: 'He supposes sadness of himself'.

What occurs, then, when the person *considers* his attributing sadness to himself? He considers his having the following property: being an x such that x attributes sadness to x. This property does not involve a concept of *himself*, for it is a property that many persons can have at once—that is to say, there can be many things x such that x attributes sadness to x.

But the concept of being an x such that x attributes sadness to x *does* involve the concept of something that attributes sadness to itself. And this latter concept, it must be conceded, *is* a concept of *a* self.

How, then, did the person get this concept of a self?

We find the answer if we consider the parallel question: 'How did the person get the concept of sadness'? To this question, the best possible answer would seem to be: 'By having it'. For sadness is a self-presenting property.

How did the person get the concept of being an x such that x attributes sadness to x? Here, once again, the best answer would seem to be: 'By having it'. For being an x such that x attributes sadness to x is also a self-presenting property.

But isn't there still more to 'self-consciousness'? We have not yet completed our account of the *unity* of consciousness.

How Many Subjects?

One may ask: 'Is it possible that what I call my experience has *several* subjects?' Writing on the first person, Elizabeth Anscombe asks: 'How, even, could one justify the assumption, if it is an assumption, that there is just one thinking which is this thinking of this thought that I am thinking, just one thinker? How do I know that "I" is not ten thinkers thinking in unison?'[8] Might not there be, for example, one person who is doing what I call my seeing and a second person who is doing what I call my hearing?

The answer lies in the fact of the unity of consciousness.

Let us consider a passage from Franz Brentano—from the chapter entitled 'The Unity of Consciousness', in his *Psychology from an Empirical Standpoint*:

> When someone thinks of and desires something, or when he thinks of several objects at the same time, he is conscious not only of different activities, but also of their simultaneity. When someone hears a melody he recognizes that he has a presentation of one note as occurring now and of other notes as having already occurred. When a person is aware of seeing and hearing, he is also aware that he is doing both at the same time. Now if we find the perception of seeing in one thing and the perception of hearing in another, in which of these things do we find the perception of their simultaneity? Obviously, in neither of them. It is clear, rather, that the inner cognition of one and the inner cognition of the other must belong to the same real unity.[9]

Brentano is telling us simply that, when a person is aware that he is seeing something and also aware that he is hearing something, then he is also aware that he is both hearing something and seeing something. Could we perhaps settle for less—say that the person who sees something and hears something is aware that the seeing and the hearing are 'parts of the same consciousness' or that they are 'compresent in consciousness'? I think not. What could it mean to say they are 'parts of the same consciousness' or 'co-present in consciousness' other than that the same person is aware of both?

Let us now attempt to make a precise statement of the principle of the unity of consciousness.

The Unity of Consciousness and Certainty

The passage from Brentano suggests the following principle: 'For every x, if it is certain for x that he is F and if it is certain for x that he is G, then (i) x is F and G and (ii) it is certain for x that he is F and G'. If we were to affirm such a principle, then we would be saying that one's self-presenting properties all present themselves as belonging to one and the same thing. This fact is doubtless at the basis of what Kant called 'the transcendental unity of apperception'.[10] But the principle would seem to be too strong.

Let us recall Kant's suggestion that the subject *need* not unite representations into a single consciousness, but should merely be such that he *could* so unite them—or, as we might say, that he should be in a position so to unite them.[11] What does it mean to say that the subject is '*in a position* so to unite them'? Perhaps the answer is this: 'In order to see that the representatives are united, the subject has only to ask himself *whether* they are united'. And what is it for the representations to *be* thus united?

I suggest that we may formulate the *principle of the unity of consciousness* as an additional material epistemic principle:

> EP4 For every x, if (i) it is certain for x that he is F and certain for x that he is G, and if (ii) x considers the question whether he is both F and G, then it is certain for x that he is both F and G.

Given what we have said about propositional certainty, we may add that, if it is certain for a subject that he is both F and G, then the *proposition* that there is something that is both F and G is one that is certain for him.

The unity of consciousness gives us a means by which we can identify without recourse to a middle term and without appeal to a set of common properties. If there is a property G which is self-presenting to me and if there is a property H which is also self-presenting to me, then, *ipso facto*, I can be certain that I have both G and H. And if I can be certain that I have both G and H, then I can also be certain of the proposition that there *is* something having both G and H.

The person's self-presenting properties, then, are such that he can be absolutely certain that they are all had by one and the same thing—namely, himself. And this is the closest he comes —and can come—to apprehending himself directly. But this awareness that there is something having the properties in question is what constitutes our basis, at any time, for all the other things that we may be said to know at that time.

We asked above: What is meant and presupposed by saying that hearing and seeing are part of the same consciousness? Kant would say that hearing and seeing have been 'united in a single consciousness'. But I think it would be clearer if we put the matter this way: One has been able to identify a subject of hearing with a subject of seeing. And one has done this without recourse to a middle term and without appeal to any set of common properties.

And so let us return to the question: 'How do I know that "I" is not ten thinkers thinking in unison'? The answer, I would say, is this: We know it in the same way as we know that there is at least one thinker.

Self-Consciousness

What more is there to self-consciousness? We are not here asking about one's psychological insight into one's own character and motivations or about the way one thinks one seems to others. We are asking a philosophical question about the sense in which a person may be said to be the object of his own awareness.

There are two senses in which one might be said to be the

object of his own awareness. In the first sense, self-consciousness or self-awareness means simply self-attribution or self-presentation—either the direct attribution of a property to oneself or one's direct awareness that one has a certain property. In this sense of the term, presumably *any* conscious being can be said to be aware of himself. But to have self-consciousness in the second sense of the term it is not enough that one attribute a property to oneself or that one be directly aware that one has a certain property. One must also 'know and believe that he, himself is the one to whom he attributes such properties'; he must recognize these attributes '*as* his own'.[12]

Can we do justice to this distinction?

There are many references in literature to a discovery that people sometimes make in childhood—a discovery which seems to be of first importance but which can be put only in some such sentence as 'I am me'.[13] What is it that is discovered in such cases? Consider the following observation by Jean Paul Richter:

I shall never forget what I have never revealed to anyone, the phenomenon which accompanied the birth of my consciousness of self [*Selbstbewusstsein*] and of which I can specify both the place and the time. One morning, as a very young child, I was standing in our front door and was looking over to the wood pile on the left, when suddenly the inner vision 'I am a me' [*ich bin ein Ich*] shot down before me like a flash of lightning from the sky, and ever since it has remained with me luminously: at that moment my ego [*Ich*] had seen itself for the first time, and for ever. One can hardly conceive of deceptions of memory in this case, since no one else's reporting could mix additions with such an occurrence, which happened merely in the curtained holy of holies of man and whose novelty alone had lent permanence to such everyday concomitants.[14]

I believe we are now able to say what the discovery in question is. It is the discovery one makes when one is first aware of the unity of consciousness; it is thus a discovery about those things one has been directly attributing to oneself. One suddenly becomes aware of the fact that they are all being attributed to the *same* thing. One realizes that there is a single thing that has all one's self-presenting properties and that *that* is the thing to which one makes all one's direct attributions. And *how* does one come to see this? It would be correct to say: 'One has only to consider it to see that it is true'. But it is, apparently, something that many people never happen to consider.

Notes

1 Other basic principles are set forth in the Second Edition of my book *Theory of Knowledge* (Englewood Cliffs, N.J., Prentice-Hall, Inc., 1976), 138–9. The principles are there restricted to the *de dicto* form, but their analogues for direct attribution are obvious.
2 See the Introduction to his *Analogy*; in *The Whole Works of Bishop Butler* (London: Thomas Teggs, 1839), p. xxxiv.
3 This distinction was proposed by Guido Küng, in a paper entitled 'Understanding and Rational Justification', *Dialectica*, Vol. III (1979), 217–32; see p. 227.
4 *Principles of Philosophy*, Part I, Principle IX; in E. S. Haldane and G. R. T. Ross, eds., *Philosophical Works of Descartes* (Cambridge: The University Press, 1931), p. 222.
5 Compare William P. Alston, 'Two Types of Foundationalism', *The Journal of Philosophy*, 73 (1976), pp. 165–85, esp. p. 170, and Ernest Sosa, 'The Foundations of Foundationalism,' forthcoming in *Nous*.
6 *Critique of Pure Reason*, B131–2; N. Kemp Smith translation, pp. 152–3.
7 A355; Kemp Smith translation, p. 337.
8 Elizabeth Anscombe, 'The First Person', in Samuel Guttenplan, ed., *Mind and Language: Wolfson College Lectures 1974* (Oxford: The Clarendon Press, 1975), pp. 45–65; the quotation is on page 58.
9 Franz Brentano, *Psychology from an Empirical Standpoint* (London: Routledge and Kegan Paul, 1973), p. 160.
10 See the *Critique of Pure Reason* A98–130, A345–9; B131–8. But Kant uses one or the other of these two types of formulation: (i) 'all representations belong to a single consciousness'; (ii) 'all of the representations experienced by any given subject belong to a single consciousness.' Presumably the former sentence is false if taken literally; hence it should be taken to say that all representations *of a given subject* belong to a single consciousness.
11 'The thought that the representations given in intuition one and all belong to me, is therefore equivalent to the thought that I unite them in self-consciousness, or can at least so unite them.'
13 Dieter Henrich, 'Zwei Theorien zur Verteidigung von Selbstbewusstsein', *Grazer Philosophische Studien*, VII (1979).
14 For an account of this experience and for some literary references to it, see Herbert Spiegelberg, 'On the "I-am-me" Experience in Childhood and Adolescence', in *Psychologia: An International Journal of Psychology in the Orient*, IV (1961), pp. 135–46.
15 'Aus Jean Pauls Leben,' *Sämtliche Werke* (Berlin: 1862), XXXIV, p. 26; quoted and translated by Spiegelberg, *op. cit.*, p. 135.

Chapter 8

TRANSCENDENT EVIDENCE AND PERCEPTION

Introduction

IF the foundation of our knowledge consists of certain subjective —or 'Cartesian'—apprehensions, and if all belief, ultimately, is a matter of self-attribution, how is it possible for a person to have knowledge about anything *other* than himself? Or, more briefly: How is transcendent evidence possible? Here we have what might be called the epistemic side of the problem of objective reference.

To deal with the problem, I shall formulate certain additional material principles of the theory of evidence, or epistemology. These principles are analogous to the principles of logic and the principles of moral philosophy.

'But', one may object, 'do we have a real problem here? You ask how "transcendent evidence" is possible. To answer your question, we have only to consider what we perceive, what we remember having perceived and what we are told by others. Then, by applying the logical principles of induction, probability and explanation to such data, we are able to know whatever it is we do know about that which "transcends" the immediate data of self-presentation. There is no need to look for any special "epistemic" principles.'

The procedure described would leave us with our problem. The question now becomes: *How* is it possible for perception and memory to provide us with information transcending the immediate data of self-presentation? Or, if we *define* perception and memory, epistemically, as that which does provide us such information, then our question becomes: How are perception and memory possible?

In this chapter, I shall consider the question of transcendent evidence only in so far as it pertains to perception.

Appearing and Being Appeared To

We have used the concept of indirect attribution to throw light upon a number of philosophical questions—including questions about the meaning of demonstratives and proper names. We now apply it to similar problems involving the nature of perception. For we may say that perception is, essentially, the indirect attribution of a property to a thing, the thing being considered *as* the thing that is appearing in a certain way.

We begin, then, with appearing.

The requisite sense of 'appear' is both causal and psychological. Traditionally, one had spoken of 'sensations' instead of 'ways of appearing'. One had said that the object of perception, acting upon the perceiver's sense-organs, caused him to 'have certain sensations'. But I would prefer to say that the object of perception causes him to *sense* in a certain way. The subject who was said to experience a red sensation does not stand in a sentient relation to an *object* which is a red sensation; rather, he is sentient *in a certain way*—a way that we could describe as 'redly'. (Compare 'he experiences sadness' and 'He feels sad': the former suggests, misleadingly, that sadness is one of two things that are related by experiencing; the latter suggests, more accurately, that being sad is a *way* of experiencing.) For philosophical purposes it is convenient to use 'is appeared to' in place of 'senses'.

Let us note the distinction between (a) 'There exists a y such that y appears to x in a certain way' and (b) 'x is appeared to (senses) in a certain way'. The first implies something about an external stimulus object; it tells us, in part, that y, acting as a stimulus object, causes the subject to be in a certain sentient state. But the second implies nothing about an external object, and tells us only about the state of the subject. In cases of phantasy, dreaming and hallucination, the second may be true while the first is false. For then one will be sensing—one will be appeared to—in a certain way, even though no external stimulus object is causing one to sense in that way.

The expression 'being appeared redly to', as we shall interpret it, must *not* be interpreted as having the same sense as any of the following expressions: 'being appeared to by something that is red'; 'being appeared to in the way in which one is normally appeared to by things that are red'; or 'being appeared to in the way in which one believes that red things normally appear'. The expression 'being appeared redly to' has what I have called its *non-comparative* sense in this use.[1]

'Being appeared redly to', in this non-comparative use, refers to a property that is self-presenting in the sense that we have defined. That is to say, being appeared redly to is necessarily such that, if a person is appeared redly to and if he considers his being appeared redly to, then he will attribute to himself the property of being appeared redly to. This use of 'being appeared redly to' is 'non-comparative', since the sense of the expression, in this use, is not *logically* connected with the sense that the word 'red' when physical things are said to be red.

Can we, then, define 'y appears redly to x' in terms of being appeared redly to and certain causal concepts? Here we must presuppose the concept of *functional dependence*: if y appears in a certain way to x, then the way x is appeared to will be functionally dependent upon the nature of y. That is to say, y will be so related to x, that, merely by varying y continuously with respect to certain of its properties, one can vary continuously the way in which x is appeared to. More specifically, if y is appearing visually to x, then y has properties which are such that, by varying them, one can vary the way in which x is visually appeared to, and analogously for the other sense-modalities.

The functional dependence that relates the appearing object and the way of being appeared to is also *structural*, since it essentially involves different *parts* of the object that appears. If, for the moment, we permit ourselves the sense-datum language ('He senses a red appearance') instead of the language of being appeared to ('He is appeared to redly'), we can easily describe this structural relation. The appearance is divisible into parts which correspond to different parts of the thing that presents the appearance. The table-top, for example, may present a uniform visual appearance; yet by varying the colour, say, of the left half of the table-top we can vary the colour of the left half of the visual appearance. (If we restrict ourselves to the language of being appeared to, we cannot thus speak of the 'parts' of a way of being appeared to, but we can distinguish various *aspects* of the way of being appeared to and we can put our point by reference to them.)

The *medium* in which an object appears will also affect the way in which the subject is appeared to. Indeed continuous variations in the former may produce continuous variations in the latter. But the medium will not have to the way of being appeared to the kind of structural relation we have referred to.

Perhaps we can distinguish the status of the *sense-organ* from that of the corresponding appearance by saying this: the nature of the appearance is *directly* dependent upon the state of the sense-organ; and it is *indirectly* dependent upon the state of that physical thing upon which the state of the sense-organ is directly dependent.

Several Senses of Perception

'Perception', in its ordinary use, is an epistemic term. If I can be said, in this ordinary sense, to perceive that there is a sheep in the field, then it is *evident* to me that there is a sheep in the field. Since our present concern is with the question, 'How is transcendent evidence possible?', we shall not begin with this epistemic sense of perception. Instead, we shall try to disentangle the epistemic and non-epistemic features of perception and then single out those processes *in virtue of which* we can be said, in this ordinary epistemic sense, to perceive—those processes upon which perceptual evidence may be said to supervene. We shall ask: What is there about those processes that makes transcendent evidence possible? And then, having an answer to this question, we can turn to the ordinary sense of perception.

The objective reference that is involved in perception does not differ in principle from what we have considered already. As we have said, perception may be characterized as a special type of direct attribution—one that essentially involves the concept of *appearance*. But there are several senses of perception to be distinguished.

An explicit formulation of a perceptual judgment will always make a reference to the perceiver himself. What one perceives is, not merely something red or something round, but that something red or something round stands in a certain relation to *oneself*. What would the relation be?

If I perceive a thing, then, of course, the thing is related to me as being one of the objects of my perception. And presumably, for each thing that I perceive, I perceive it in *some* way or other that distinguishes my perception of *that* thing at that time from my perception of any other thing at that time. But *this* cannot be the identifying relation that is involved in perception. What one *perceives* is not, in the first instance, that one perceives an object in a certain way. The fact of perception is not a part of the content of perception.

The identifying relation that is involved in perception pertains, rather, to the concept of *appearing*. If I perceive a thing, then I judge that there is just one thing that is appearing to me in a certain way. I may judge, for example, that something appears red to me. If many things are such that each one is appearing red to me, then for each of them there will be a further way of appearing which is such that that thing is the sole thing that is appearing to me in *that* way. One thing might appear red and round, another thing red and square, and so on.

Our first sense of perception, then, may be characterized as follows:

(I) The property of being F is such that x perceptually takes y to have it = Df. There is a way of appearing such that y and only y appears in that way to x; and the property of being F is a sensible property that x indirectly attributes to y, as the thing that appears to him in that way.

Sensible properties are those properties that Locke called 'secondary qualities.'

This primary sense of perception is a very broad sense, for it does not imply evidence or veridicality. From the fact that one thus perceptually takes a thing to be F, it does not follow that the thing *is* F, nor does it follow that the perceiver has *evidence* that the thing is F.

Given this primary sense of perception, we may now define the expression, 'x perceives y'. Let us say:

(II) x perceives y = Df. There is a property which is such that x perceptually takes y to have it.

Let us call this the *non-propositional* sense of perception. I assume that the sub-species of such perception—seeing, hearing, tasting, feeling—can be described by reference to the kinds of ways of being appeared to that they involve.[2] Still other senses of perception ('He heard the concert', 'He saw the shadow move') could readily be singled out.[3] But these are not relevant to our present concern.

The two senses of perception just defined presuppose what we may call the *self-presenting* sense of perception:

(III) The property of being F is such that x perceptually takes there to be something that has it = Df. x is appeared to in a way which is such that he directly attributes to himself the property of being appeared to in that way by something that is F.

The definiendum may also be read as 'x perceptually takes there to be something that is F'.

Although perception, in this third sense, implies that the subject is being appeared to in a certain way, it does not imply that anything is *appearing* to him in that way. This last fact is our excuse for using the awkward locution 'he perceptually takes *there to be* something that has it', instead of the simpler 'he perceptually takes something to have it'.

The several senses of perception here distinguished do not yet include the familiar 'perceives that' locution of ordinary language—as in 'He perceives that someone is approaching', or 'He perceives someone to be approaching'. We will be in a position to explicate this ordinary sense of perception after we have formulated certain further epistemic principles.

The Epistemically Unsuspect

In the previous chapter we set forth a number of material epistemic principles. The first of these pertained to the self-presenting properties that are sometimes said to constitute the foundation for the rest of what we know. The importance of such foundations should not lead us to neglect another moment of epistemic justification, which is not in the same sense foundational.

The term 'foundation', in its application to knowledge, suggests that our knowledge is comparable to a building or to a pyramid. But a different metaphor has been proposed by Otto Neurath. He said that our knowledge is to be compared with a ship or a raft, and that the epistemologist is to be compared with a sailor 'who, unable to return to dock, must reconstruct his vessel on the open sea, and is therefore forced to make use of the best constituents that are at hand'.[4] We have here two quite different ways of looking at knowledge. Must we choose between 'the pyramid and the raft'?[5]

The figure of the pyramid suggests that we can use material

that is solid, firm and absolutely reliable, and that of the raft suggests that we must settle for what is at best makeshift and haphazard. But perhaps *both* figures are accurate. I suggest that we do not have here two different conceptions of knowledge. What we have—metaphors aside—are two different aspects of our knowledge, each of them of fundamental importance. There are two moments of epistemic justification, one of them foundational and the other not.

In considering what it is that we are justified in believing we should take into account, not only that which is objectively certain and thus foundational for our subject at any given time, but also certain things which may then be said to have *some presumption in their favour* for him. I have said that the direct attribution of a property has some presumption in its favour for a given subject at a given time, provided that the direct attribution of that property is then more reasonable for him than is the direct attribution of its negation. Let us now consider such attributions and see how they function in our general epistemic principles.

To locate that which has some presumption in its favour, I shall propose an additional material epistemic principle—and one which is extremely latitudinarian. This is the principle that *anything* we find ourselves believing may be said to have *some* presumption in its favour—*provided* it is not explicitly contradicted by the set of other things that we believe. The principle may be thought of as an instance of a more general truth—that it is reasonable to put our trust in our own cognitive faculties unless we have some positive ground for questioning them.

The principle is this:

> EP5 For every x, if (i) x directly attributes to himself the property of being F, and if (ii) x being F is not explicitly contradicted by the set of properties that x directly attributes to x, then his being F has some presumption in its favour for x.

The principle is readily extended to propositional belief. Thus we may say that, for every x, if x accepts a proposition or state of affairs that is not explicitly contradicted by any conjunction of propositions each such that it is accepted by x, then that proposition has some presumption in its favour for x. (One proposition 'explicitly contradicts' another provided only that it *entails* the negation of the other; the relation between properties is analogous.

In affirming EP5 we follow Carneades, who assigned a positive epistemic status to 'the uncontradicted'.[6] The apparent over-permissiveness of this principle can be corrected by reference to a certain subset of these 'uncontradicted' attributions; this subset constitutes our next category.

From among the attributes that thus have some presumption in their favour for our subject, we may now single out those that are 'epistemically unsuspect' or 'epistemically in the clear'. An attribution of a property P may be said to be *epistemically unsuspect*, or *epistemically in the clear*, for any subject, provided only that it is *not disconfirmed* by the set of 'uncontradicted' properties we have just singled out. More exactly, a property P is epistemically in the clear for a given subject provided it is not disconfirmed by the set of those properties other than P that have some presumption in their favour for him, and analogously for propositions or states of affairs. (If a proposition e thus 'confirms' a proposition h, then necessarily, for every x, if e is x's total evidence, then h has some presumption in its favour for x, and analogously for properties.)

According to our latitudinarian epistemic principle EP5, anything we believe has some presumption in its favour provided it is not explicitly contradicted by anything else we believe. Given the concept of the epistemically unsuspect, we may formulate an additional principle which will compensate for this permissiveness of EP5. We will equate the epistemically unsuspect with that which is epistemically *acceptable*. (We have said that the direct attribution of a property is 'acceptable' provided that withholding that property is not more reasonable than attributing that property. And, analogously, a proposition is acceptable provided that withholding it is not more reasonable than accepting it.)

Our sixth principle, then, is this:

EP6 For every x, and every property H, the direct attribution of H is epistemically in the clear for x if and only if it is epistemically acceptable for x.

Analogously, a proposition is epistemically in the clear for x if and only if it is acceptable for x. The principle thus tells us that anything that is epistemically in the clear is epistemically acceptable, but it also tells us that nothing is epistemically acceptable unless it is epistemically in the clear.

Our new principle thus enables us to single out, from the set of beliefs having some presumption in their favour, a subset of beliefs which are also epistemically acceptable.

We are now in a position to formulate our principles of perceptual evidence. These will all make reference to that which is epistemically acceptable, or in the clear.

The Principles of Perceptual Evidence

We begin with a simple appearance principle. What we have a right to affirm, I suggest, is a generalization upon the following: *'Being appeared redly* to tends to make it evident to the subject that *there is something that appears red to him'*. In other words, if a person is appeared redly to, then it is evident to him that there *is* something that appears red to him—provided that he considers the question of whether something is appearing red to him and provided that he has no reason to suppose that it is *not* the case that something appears red to him.

We may now generalize our principle as follows:

> EP7 For every x, if there is a way of appearing which is such that (i) it is self-presenting and (ii) x is appeared to in that way, then the following is evident for x provided it is epistemically in the clear for him and something that he considers: there is something that is appearing that way to him.

Being thus appeared to puts one in contact, so to speak, with external reality, and such initial contact, it would seem, can be only via appearances.

A simple principle of perceptual evidence would be illustrated by the following: If a person perceptually takes there to be a sheep in the field before him, then it is *evident* to him that there is a sheep in the field. Thus Meinong had held, in effect, that the fact that we *think* we perceive confers 'presumptive evidence [*Vermutungsevidenz*]' upon the proposition or state of affairs which is the object of our ostensible perception.[7] And H. H. Price has said that the fact that we 'perceptually accept' a certain proposition is sufficient to confer some positive epistemic status on that proposition. Price put this point as follows: 'We want to be able to say: the fact that a material thing is perceptually presented to the mind is *prima facie evidence* of the thing's existence and of its really having that sort of surface which it ostensibly has: or, again, that there is *some presumption in favour of* this, not merely in the sense that we do as a matter of fact presume it (which of course we do) but in the sense that we are entitled to do so'.[8] But such principles, as they stand, are somewhat over-permissive, epistemically.

Using the concept of the 'epistemically unsuspect', or of that which is 'epistemically in the clear', we might say that certain perceptual attributions are beyond reasonable doubt—*provided* they are epistemically unsuspect. In this way we could formulate a principle that is less permissive than those proposed by Meinong and Price. But we could add that, if such an attribution is a member of a set of properties, which mutually support each other and each of which is beyond reasonable doubt, then the attribution is evident. (We may say that the members of a set of two or more properties 'mutually support' each other provided each of the properties is such that the conjunction of all the others tends to confirm it and is logically independent of it.)

This, then, is our perceptual principle:

EP8 For any subject x, if (i) x perceptually takes there to be something which is f, and if (ii) his perceiving something which is F is epistemically in the clear for x, then it is beyond reasonable doubt for x that he perceives something which is F. If, moreover, his perceiving something which is F is a member of a set of properties, which mutually support each other and each of which is beyond reasonable doubt for x, then it is evident for x that he perceives something which is F.

Let us note certain features of this principle. The first part of the antecedent of the first part of the principle ('x perceptually takes there to be something which is F') refers to the 'self-presenting sense of perception' singled out above. The second part of the antecedent ('his perceiving something which is F is epistemically in the clear') pertains to the class of things we singled out by means of principle EP6. The consequent of the first part of the principle refers to the 'non-propositional sense of perception' also singled out above.

The consequent of the first part of the principle reads: 'it is evident for *x* that he *perceives something which is F.*' We should remind ourselves that one can perceive something which is F without thereby perceiving the thing *to be* F—without thereby perceiving *that* the thing is F. Thus if the person that I see is a thief, then I perceive something which is a thief. But even if I know that he is a thief, it is not likely that I *perceive* him to be a thief—it is not likely that, in any sense, I perceive *that* he is a thief.

Our principle EP8 states certain conditions under which we may say of a person that it is evident or beyond reasonable doubt for him that he perceives something which is F. It does not enable us to say, *de re*, of that person and any external object *y*, that it is beyond reasonable doubt for the person that he perceives that *that* particular thing *y* is F. In other words, our principle entitles us to say: '*x* perceives that there is a *y* such that *y* is F', but not: 'there exists a *y* such that S perceives that *y* is F'. It may be self-presenting for *x* that he is *being appeared to* in a certain way (that he *senses* in a certain way). But it cannot be self-presenting for him that there *is* something that *is appearing* to him in that way (i.e., it cannot be self-presenting to him that an external stimulus object *causes* him to sense in that way).

By means of what principle, then, can the person pass from a way of appearing to a particular physical thing that 'transcends' that way of appearing? We are looking for a principle which enables us to say with respect to two things, *x* and *y*, that it is evident to *x* that *y* is F. We can find such a principle if we look to that which is self-presenting and also to that which is epistemically in the clear.

I propose, then, the following principle:

EP9 For every *x* and *y*, if (i) *x* perceptually takes *y* and only *y* to be F, and if (ii) it is epistemically in the clear for *x* that he perceives something which is *f*, then *y* is such that it is beyond reasonable doubt for *x* that it is F; and if it is evident for *x* that he perceives something which is F, then *y* is such that it is evident for *x* that it is F.

In the first clause of the antecedent we refer to the primary sense of perception, and in the second to the non-propositional sense of perception.

This final perceptual principle introduces the *de re* epistemic locution: 'y is such that it is evident to x that it is F'. Therefore the principle is, in a certain respect, less pure than the preceding principle, EP8. For, in theory at least, one can ascertain merely by reflection whether or not the antecedent condition of EP8 obtains. But the present principle, EP9, is not applicable unless there is an external physical thing which is causing the subject to sense in the way that he does. And this fact cannot be ascertained merely by reflection. It cannot be self-presenting to the subject that there *is* a certain thing which he perceives to be F; it can be self-presenting only that he *perceptually takes* there to be something that is F. Hence we might call EP9 a 'quasi-epistemic principle'.

Our perceptual principles are instances of the more general truth: 'It is reasonable to trust the senses until one has positive reason for distrusting them'.[9]

'But it's at least logically possible that our senses as well as our memories always deceive us. If that were in fact the case, *then* would it be reasonable to trust the senses?' The answer will be suggested by a comparable question: 'It is logically possible that all our inductive conclusions (strictly speaking, those that are logically contingent) are false. In such a case, would it be reasonable to follow the principles of induction?' I am convinced that, in such a case, it *would* be reasonable to follow them.

The Ordinary Epistemic Sense of Perception

We are now in a position to explicate the ordinary epistemic sense of perception, as expressed in such locutions as 'x perceives that y is F' and 'x perceives y to be F'. It is this:

(IV) x perceives y to be F = Df. y is F; x perceptually takes y to be F; and it is evident to x that y is F.

Alternative readings of the definiendum are: 'x perceives that y is F' and: 'the property of being F is such that x perceives y to have it'. The second clause in the definiens—'x perceptually takes y to be F'—refers to what we called the primary sense of perception. This primary sense was defined by reference to appearing and indirect attribution. The final clause in the definiens—'it is evident to x that y is F'—was defined in the previous chapter in terms of epistemic preferability, and we have seen in principles EP8 and EP9 the conditions under which the final clause may be said to be true.

We consider, finally, the nature of negative perception.

Negative Perception

The senses of perception that we have set forth may not seem to provide for the possibility of negative perception. What, then, is the epistemological status of such reports as the following?

(1) 'I don't seem to see a dog.'

(2) 'I don't take there to be a dog.'

(3) 'Nothing is such that I take it to be a dog.'

(4) 'I don't see that there are dogs here.'

(5) 'I don't see any dogs.'

(6) 'I see that there are not any dogs here.'

It is sometimes said that there is no negative perception. Franz Brentano wrote, for example: 'Our perceptions are all positive; none of them is negative'.[10] According to him, such negative judgments involve the *a priori* knowledge of what he had called 'the laws of positive opposition'—e.g., that nothing can be both red and blue, and that nothing can be both circular and angular.[11] Let us consider this thesis in application to the list we have just made.

Those negative perceptual judgments that pertain to external reality—in particular, (5) and (6)—would seem to require such a judgment of incompatibility. One reasons, in effect: 'Given what I do see, there could hardly be any dogs here'.

Does all negative apprehension thus involve judgments of incompatibility—or is there a more direct type of negative apprehension? Russell has suggested that the latter is the case: 'It seems that we must conclude that pure negative propositions can be empirically known without being inferred. "Listen. Do you hear anything?" "No."'[12] And I would say that he is right.

The subjective negative judgments that are suggested by (1)

and (2) above—i.e., 'I don't seem to see a dog' and 'I don't take anything to be a dog'—are apparently direct and not derived from judgments of incompatibility. When I make such a judgment, I don't do so on the basis of finding myself in a positive state which excludes my taking there to be something that is a dog.

Taking there to be a dog is self-presenting in the sense that we have set forth. Hence, if what I have said is correct, *not* taking there to be a dog may also be self-presenting. If I do not take there to be a dog, and if I ask myself whether it is the case that I do not take there to be a dog, then I will attribute to myself the property of not taking there to be a dog.

When a person thus makes a negative judgment which is not based upon a judgment of incompatibility, he reflects upon his own psychological state ('Do I see any dogs?'). I believe we may say, therefore, that all such negative perception involves reference to our own intentional attitudes. Whitehead had inferred from this fact that, strictly speaking, *consciousness* first arises in the case of negative perception: 'The general case of conscious perception is the negative perception . . . Consciousness is the feeling of negation'.[13] But, given our characterization of consciousness in terms of the self-presenting, it would be more accurate to say that negative perception, unlike affirmative perception, always involves what Leibniz called 'apperception' —an awareness of some one of one's own intentional attitudes.

Let us consider our list once again. In the case of (1) and (2), we have direct negative perceptions. In the case of (3), we have a judgment about external reality ('Everything is such that I do not take it to be a dog'), which is justified by a direct negative perception. And the same direct negative perception justifies (4). But (5) and (6), as we have said, are indirect, requiring a judgment of incompatibility.

Conclusion

Once we are given a corpus of epistemic principles, we can go on to apply the principles of induction and of the theory of probability and explanation. But the application of such further principles presupposes a body of evidence of the sort that we have singled out. The perceptual principles I have formulated have their analogues for memory and also, I believe, for 'the problem of other minds' and what is sometimes called 'hermeneutics'. But these topics are beyond the scope of the present study.

Now we may complete our account of objective reference.

Notes

1 See the chapter called 'Three Uses of Appear Words', in my book *Perceiving: A Philosophical Study* (Ithaca: Cornell University Press, 1957), pp. 43–53: the distinction is further defended in 'Comments and Replies', *Philosophia*. VII (1978), pp. 599–602.
2 See Franz Brentano, *Untersuchungen zur Sinnespsychologie*, Second Edition (Hamburg: Felix Meiner Verlag, 1979), pp. 157–63; compare H. P. Grice, 'Some Remarks about the Senses', in R. J. Butler, ed., *Analytic Philosophy*, First Series (Oxford: Basil Blackwell, 1963), pp. 133–53.
3 Compare Fred Dretske, *Seeing and Knowing* (Chicago: University of Chicago Press, 1969), p. 23.
4 Otto Neurath, 'Protokollsätze', *Erkenntnis*, Band III (1932–1933), pp. 204–14; the quotation is on p. 206.
5 Compare Ernest Sosa, 'The Raft and the Pyramid', *Midwest Studies in Philosophy*, V (1980). Sosa makes clear that the two figures do not exclude each other.
6 Compare *Sextus Empiricus*, Volume II, Loeb Classical Library (London: William Heinemann, Ltd., 1933), p. 95; 'Against the Logicians', 1, pp. 176–7. Compare the following definition proposed by John Pollock: 'P is *prima facie* justified for S' means: "It is necessarily true that if S believes (or were to believe) that P, and S has no reason for thinking that it is false that P, then S is (or would be) justified in believing that P".' John Pollock, *Knowledge and Justification* (Princeton: Princeton University Press, 1972), p. 30.
7 See A. Meinong, *Über die Erfahrungsgrundlagen unseres Wissens* (1906), published in A. Meinong, *Gesamtausgabe*, Band V (Graz: Akademische Druck- und Verlagsanstalt, 1973); see esp. pp. 398–404.
8 H. H. Price, *Perception* (New York: Robert M. McBride & Company, 1935), p. 185.
9 Compare Bertrand Russell: '. . . beliefs caused by perception are to be accepted unless there are positive grounds for rejecting them'. *An Inquiry into Meaning and Truth* (New York: W. W. Norton & Company, 1940), p. 166.
10 *Versuch über die Erkenntnis* (Hamburg: Felix Meiner Verlag, 1970), p. 10.
11 *Op. cit.*, p. 10. Compare Russell, *The Principles of Mathematics* (Cambridge: The University Press, 1903), p. 167: 'It is such synthetic judgments of incompatibility that lead to negative judgments . . .' Compare also Russell's *An Inquiry into Meaning and Truth*, pp. 100–101.
12 *An Inquiry into Meaning and Truth*, p. 203.
13 A. N. Whitehead, *Process and Reality* (Cambridge: The University Press, 1930), p. 235; compared pp. 272, 417–18.

Chapter 9
KNOWLEDGE AND BELIEF *DE RE*

A Problem of Interpretation

WE are in a position, finally, to consider the nature of *de re* knowledge and belief, and in particular the relation of attribution, as we have conceived it, to such knowledge and belief. Our question is: Is there more to *de re* belief than mere attribution, direct or indirect, and if so, what?

We begin, then, by recalling our definition of *indirect attribution*:

D1 y is such that, as the thing to which x bears R, x indirectly attributes to it the property of being F = Df. x bears R to y and only to y; and x directly attributes to x a property which entails the property of bearing R to just one thing and to a thing that is F.

An alternative reading for the definiens was: 'x indirectly attributes to y, under the description, *the thing to which he bears R*, the property of being F'. We also introduced the following abbreviated locution:

D2 y is such that x indirectly attributes to it the property of being F = Df. There is a relation R such that x indirectly attributes to y, as the thing to which x bears R, the property of being F.

Shall we now characterize *de re* belief by reference to attribution which is either direct or indirect? in such a case we would be saying this: y is believed by a to be F, if and only if, a directly or indirectly attributes to y the property of being F.

From one point of view, this conception of *de re* belief may seem to be excessively latitudinarian. It requires us to say that, for the tallest spy to be believed by me to be a spy, it is enough that there be one spy taller than all the others and that I directly attribute to myself the property of being such that there is one spy who is taller than all the others. Is it *that* simple for me to make him the object of my belief?

There would seem to be two quite different reactions to this question. Some feel that in such a situation the tallest spy *is* believed by me to be a spy. Thus Sosa notes that, if I have a belief I would express by saying 'The tallest spy is red-headed', then one can truly say to the tallest spy: 'You are believed by him to be red-headed'.[1] He adds that, if the police have no important clues but think that the one who robbed the bank has fled to Chicago, then one may say to the one who robbed the bank: 'Now the police think that you fled to Chicago'. Such facts as these seem to suggest that it is relatively easy for the tallest spy and the one who robbed the bank to be believed about by the rest of us.

Yet there are other considerations which suggest that any such conception of *de re* belief is excessively latitudinarian. Thus one may be reluctant to say, in the case of the first example, that there *is* someone whom I believe to be the tallest spy. Certainly, if I believe only that the tallest spy is a spy, then I do not yet have any *suspects*. And one may be reluctant to say, in the case of the second example, that there *is* anyone whom the police suspect. 'The police believe that there is someone who robbed the bank, but there isn't anyone of whom it can be said that the police believe that *he* robbed the bank.' If there are no suspects in these cases, how can it be said that there *is* someone who is the object of the respective beliefs? (Compare Quine's expression: Witold 'Has his candidate'.[2] What is it for Witold to have his candidate?)

The solution, I suggest, is that there are two very different ways of interpreting the expression 'There exists a y such that y is believed by a to be F,' and that in considering the problem of *de re* belief we tend to confuse these possible interpretations.

According to the one interpretation, 'There exists a y such that y is believed by a to be F' tells us this:

(A) There exists a y such that a directly or indirectly attributes to y the property of being F.

Taking the expression this way, we are justified in the latitudinarian observations referred to above. Thus, in the case of the first example, there *is* an x—namely, the tallest spy—such that x is believed by me to be a spy.

The second interpretation of the expression 'There exists a y such that y is believed by a to be F' is suggested by our phrase 'Now they suspect *you*'. It is also suggested by our statement above: 'The police believe that there is someone who robbed the bank, but there isn't anyone of whom it can be said that the police believe that *he* robbed the bank'. Here we are presupposing a certain degree of epistemic intimacy between the believer and the object of his belief. The presupposition might be put by saying: the believer *identifies* a certain thing *as* the thing he believes to have a certain property. Hence locution (A) above should be contrasted with the following:

(E) There exists a y such that a identifies y as a thing he believes to be F.

I cannot be said to *suspect* you of being the thief unless I can 'identify you as the one whom I believe to be a thief'. What, then, of the phrase 'a identifies y as a thing he believes to be F?'

The expression 'to identify', in our present interpretation, is epistemic. I have just said that it implies a certain degree of what we might call '*epistemic intimacy*' between the believer and the object of his attribution. In order to explicate this sense of identification, we must appeal to the concepts of the theory of knowledge that we have discussed in the previous two chapters. These concepts will enable us to explicate what is meant by formula (B). Then we shall be in a position to see that there are two different senses of *de re* belief—the latitudinarian sense that satisfies formula (A), and the more rigorous sense that satisfies formula (B).

Types of Identification

If I believe myself to have a certain property (i.e., if I directly attribute that property to myself), and if, further, I consider my believing myself to have that property, then I may be said to have identified *myself* as a thing I believe to have that property.

When can I be said to identify something *other* than myself as a thing I believe to have a certain property?

Perception illustrates our identification formula (B) above: 'There exists a y such that a identifies y as a thing he believes to be F'. The strict sense of perception, I have said, is this:

(D3) The property of being F is such that x perceives y to have it = Df. y is F; x perceptually takes y to be F; and it is evident to x that y is F.

Perceptual taking, it will be recalled, was defined as a type of indirect attribution: if I perceptually take a thing to be F, then I attribute to the thing, *as* the thing that is appearing to me in a certain way, the property of being F.

If I thus *perceive* a thing to have a certain property, then I may be said to have identified the thing *as* a thing which I *believe* to have that property. But let us be clear about the way in which our analysis applies to such cases. If I perceive one and only one thing to be approaching, and if I believe that the thing I perceive to be approaching is a sheep (that is to say, if I directly attribute to myself the property of perceiving just one thing to be approaching and of perceiving a sheep to be approaching), then, of course, I do not thereby *perceive* the thing in question to be a sheep. But I can be said, in this situation, to identify it as a thing I *believe* to be a sheep. In other words, if there is a certain property G which is such that I perceive a thing to have G, and if I directly attribute to myself the property of being such that the thing I perceive to be G is F, then I may be said to identify the thing as a thing which I believe to be F.

By means of perception, then, I can identify you as one I believe to be F—and I can do this without thereby perceiving you to be F.

Formula (B)—'There exists a y such that a identifies y as a thing he believes to be F'—holds in still other cases. To describe these other cases, we must take into consideration some of the things that the believer *knows*. A person may be said to *know* that he, himself, has a certain property provided that (i) he does have that property, (ii) it is evident to him that he has it, and (iii) he directly attributes it to himself.[3] By reference to this sense of knowing, we may further characterize the type of epistemic intimacy I may bear to you.

The identifying relation by means of which I single you out may be one such that I *know* myself to bear it to just one thing. Suppose that you are the one who robbed the bank where my savings are and I believe that the bank was robbed by just one person. I have then singled you out—in a somewhat broad sense of the expression 'singled you out'. Now suppose, further, that I also *know* that the bank where my savings are has been robbed by just one person. If the relation by means of which I single you out is one such that I know myself to bear it to just one thing, then I am closer to you, epistemically, than I would be if I were merely to believe but not to know that I bear such a relation to just one thing.

We now complicate the previous situation by making two additional assumptions. First, let us assume that there are a number of different identifying relations such that you are the thing to which I bear each of these relations; each relation involves *knowing* in the sense just described; the different relations are logically independent of each other; and my evidence in the case of any one of them is *independent* of my evidence in the case of any other. (In saying that the evidence is 'independent', I mean this: for each relation, there are certain things which are such that they make it evident for me that the relation obtains and that do not make it evident for me that the other relation obtains.[4] We might have this situation, for example, if you are, not only the one who robbed the bank where by savings are, but also the one who chairs the school committee in the town where I live.

Now let us suppose, secondly, that I *combine* such independent identifications. Thus I may find out that the two relations in question point to one and the same person. In this case I will know myself to be such that the person who robbed the bank where my savings are is that same as the person who chairs the school committee in the town where I live. In such a case I have been able to identify you as being *both* the one who robbed the bank and *also* the one who chairs the school committee. The more such relations I thus combine—provided that my evidence for the one is independent of my evidence for the other—the greater will be my epistemic proximity to you.

In this type of case, then, I directly attribute to myself two descriptions of the following sort: the first description says, of a certain relation R, that I bear R to just one thing; the second says, of a certain relation S, that I bear S to just one thing; I know myself to bear R and S to the same thing; and my evidence pertaining to R is independent of my evidence pertaining to S.

We may say that, in such a case, I have *identified* you as a thing to which, under several descriptions, I have indirectly attributed a certain property. We may define the relevant concept as follows:

(D4) x identifies y as a thing to which, under several descriptions, he indirectly attributes the property of being F = Df. (i) There is a relation R which is such that x indirectly attributes to y, as the thing to which he bears R, the property of being F; (ii) there is a relation S which is such that x indirectly attributes to y, as the thing to which he bears S, the property of being F; (iii) x knows himself to bear R and S to the same thing; and (iv) x's evidence for believing that he bears R to just one thing is independent of his evidence to believing that he bears S to just one thing.

Finally, there is still another dimension of such intimacy. We have imagined that there are many relations, each such that I know myself to bear them to the *same* thing. Suppose now that there is also a relation of this sort: I bear it only to you; I know that I bear it only to one thing; but I do *not* know that I bear it to the thing to which I bear the set of relations I have combined in the manner described above. For example, in addition to having the characteristics just discussed, you might also be the one I had breakfast with this morning. It may be that I *know* that I had breakfast with just one person this morning, and yet that I haven't combined this description of you with the others.

Indeed, where this last situation obtains, one may be tempted to say that the subject of the indirect attribution has *not* yet identified the object ('He doesn't realize who it is he had breakfast with!'). But if we thus say: 'He has not yet identified the thief', we are likely to mean that there is some description under which he *has* identified the thief but which he has not yet combined with the description of being a thief. Paradoxically, if there is such a dangling description, and if it is of special interest, then the better the subject knows the thief under these other descriptions (that is, the more such identifying relations he has combined), the greater will be the temptation to say that he has *not* identified the thief.

We are now in a position explicate the concepts involved in our locution (B) above: 'There exists a y such that a identifies y as a thing he believes to be F'.

(D5) There exists a y such that x identifies y as a thing he believes to be F = Df. The property of being F is such that either: (i) x attributes it directly to y and he considers his attributing it to y; or (ii) there is a property G such that x perceives y to be G and x attributes to himself the property of being such that the thing he perceives to be G is F; or (iii) x identifies y as a thing to which he indirectly attributes the property of being F.

It is important to remind ourselves that, no matter how well acquainted I may be with you, it is possible that, although (1) I attribute a certain property to you under one of your descriptions, nevertheless (2) there is *another* description which is such that, under that description, I attribute the negation of that property to you.

Moreover, if there is a description under which one person identifies a certain object, and under which a second person has *not* identified that object, then the first person may well say of the second that 'he has not identified the object'. But the context of such a statement will presuppose some description of the object; hence a more explicit statement would be one saying that the person has not identified the object under that description.

The Two Senses of the *De Re* Attitudes

We have said that there is a certain ambiguity in the *de re* belief locution 'There exists a y such that y is believed by a to have the property of being F.' The locution may be taken in accordance with formula (A): 'There exists a y such that a directly or indirectly attributes to y the property of being F'. Or it may be taken in accordance with formula (B): 'There exist a y such that a identifies y as a thing that he believes to be F'. We have now seen how these two interpretations are related.

How, then, are we to interpret *de re* belief? The technical expression '*de re* belief' has precisely the same ambiguity as does the locution 'There exists a y such that y is believed by a to be F'. If we interpret the expression in the one way, our theory of *de re* belief will be latitudinarian; if we interpret it in the other way, it will be more rigid.

We have seen that, when one wishes to show that it is very easy for one thing to be believed about by another, then one interprets 'believed about' in accordance with formula (A): 'There exists a y such that a directly or indirectly attributes to y the property of being F', and when one wishes to show that it is very difficult for one thing to be believed about by another, then one interprets 'believed about' in accordance with formula (E): 'There exists a y such that a identifies y as a thing he believes to be'.

Once we are clear about the possibility of ambiguity, we need not lose our way. For you to be *believed about* by me, it is necessary only that I indirectly attribute some property to you. But for you to be *identified* by me *as* one concerning whom I have certain beliefs, then it is necessary that I stand to you in the kind of epistemic intimacy we have just described.

What we have said about the two senses of *de re* belief may be applied, *mutatis mutandis*, to the other intentional attitudes, but we should note in passing that there are special problems in the case of what we have been calling *considering*—problems that are seldom, if ever, discussed.

The basic locution for considering would be: 'x directly considers y as having the property of being F'. And, as before, we would stipulate that necessarily, for every x and y, if x considers y as having a certain property, then x is identical with y.

What is it, then, for me to make *you* the object of my considering—for me to consider or think of you as having a certain property? Here, too, we may appeal to those relations which are such that I can identify you as being the one to whom I stand in those relations. If I think of myself as being such that the one I bear those relations to is F, then I can be said to think of you as having the property of being F. But the special problems that considering involves may be illustrated by two further facts: first, even though I may know that I bear the relations in question only to you, I can also think of some *other* person as being the one to whom I bear those relations (while talking with you I could think of myself as talking with someone else instead). Secondly, I could think of you as *not* being such that you are the one to whom I stand in those relations (I could be talking just with you and yet contemplate your being such that I am not talking with you). Suppose, now, that you are the one to whom I bear a certain relation R and that Jones is the one to whom I bear a certain relation S. And suppose, further, that I think of myself as being such that the one to whom I bear R is the same as the one to whom I bear S. One may ask whether, in such a case, I think of you as being the one to whom I bear S, or whether I think of Jones as being the one to whom I bear R. (It may not be helpful to say: 'I think of you as being the same person as Jones'.) Perhaps the following will suggest how such cases are to be treated: if the property I directly consider myself as having is 'epistemically closer' to you than it is to Jones, then the indirect object of my supposition is you and not Jones. (The requisite sense of this use of 'epistemically closer' may be suggested by the following. Suppose that a property I attribute to myself implies a number of independent identifying relations I bear just to you and also a number of such relations I bear just to Jones, and suppose I know that I have that property. If the number of independent identifying relations that thus point to you is greater than the number of those that point to Jones, then the property is *epistemically closer* to you than it is to Jones.)

These considerations also have their analogues in the case of *wishing*, but since our present concern is primarily with believing, I will not elaborate upon them here.

Eternal Objects and *De Re* Belief

What we have said about the distinction between the latitudinarian and the rigid sense of *de re* belief is readily applicable to belief that is directed upon contingent things. We should make certain further comments to ensure application to belief that is directed upon eternal objects.

In Chapter 4 we discussed the way in which eternal objects may be made the objects of indirect attribution. We raised the question: Does belief about eternal objects involve more than such indirect attribution? We may now answer this question.

Our conception of indirect attribution is as permissive or latitudinarian in application to eternal objects as it is in application to individual things. Consider this situation: there are nine planets; Jones believes, *de dicto*, that the number of planets is eight; and he also believes, *de dicto*, that eight is an even number. We may have to say, therefore, that Jones indirectly attributes the property of being an even number to the number nine. How, then, are we to avoid concluding that nine is believed by him to be an even number?

Let us take note, briefly, of two recent attempts to deal with this question.

David Kaplan has suggested that one cannot be said to have a belief about the number nine unless one's belief can be expressed in a sentence containing a name which 'necessarily denotes' the number nine.⁵ His account is roughly this: you can be said to believe with respect to the number nine that it is even if, and only if, there is a proper name a such that (i) a necessarily designates the number nine and (ii) the proposition expressed by the sentence which results from replacing 'x' in 'x is even' by a is one that you accept. The account thus presupposes that the type of sentence referred to expresses a proposition, but we have rejected this presupposition. Moreover, it makes use of the undefined expression 'denotes' (sometimes Kaplan uses the verb 'names' instead). Hence it attempts to explicate intentional concepts by reference to linguistic concepts: it is therefore inconsistent with our principle of the primacy of the intentional. But, since we have defined the verb 'designates', this account could be available to us—if it were otherwise satisfactory. What are we to say, however, of 'necessarily denotes'? Given what we have said about designation, there would seem to be *no* term that *necessarily* denotes the thing it denotes, and hence no term that necessarily denotes the number nine. The English word 'nine' is not necessarily such that it denotes the number nine— any more than the English word 'dog' is necessarily such that it denotes the class of dogs.

A modified version of Kaplan's view is proposed by Diana Ackerman—but one which replaces 'necessarily denote' by a reference to a *numeral*. The sentence expressing the person's *de dicto* belief is now said to contain a *numeral* that designates the number nine.⁶ This move leaves us with the question 'How is the semantic role of numerals to be distinguished from that of other types of names? How does it happen that *they* get us closer, so to speak, to the objects that they designate'?

The answer to this question—and the solution to our problem —may be found if we consider the following definition:

(D6) y is an eternal object which is such that x identifies it as the thing to which he attributes the property of being F = Df. There is a property H, a relation R, and a property C such that: x bears R to y and only to y; y is an eternal object which necessarily has C, and nothing other than y can possibly have C; H is necessarily such that whatever has it bears R to a thing that has both C and the property of being F; if the property of being F is logically implied by H, then it is entailed by H; and x directly attributes H to x.

We have used the expression 'is necessarily such that' in this definition, but we have used it only in application to eternal objects.

How is it that numerals get us so close to the things they designate? It is because each numeral has as part of its sense— *happens* to have as part of its sense—a property constituting an individual essence of the number that it designates, i.e., a property C such that the number necessarily has C and nothing else can possibly have C. Thus the numeral 'nine', unlike the descriptive phrase 'the number of planets', has as part of its sense the property of being the successor of eight—a property that nine has necessarily, and that nothing else can have. Other terms which similarly entail individual concepts of the things they designate are 'the property blue' (as distinguished from 'the colour of the sky') and 'all men being mortal' (as distinguished from 'Aristotle's favourite universal proposition').

So we may also distinguish two senses of that *de re* belief that may be directed upon eternal objects. One is that latitudinarian sense which is equivalent to indirect attribution, and the other is the more rigouristic sense outlined in the above definition.

A Test Case

Herbert Heidelberger has called attention to what he takes to be a limitation of my earlier attempt to explicate *de re* belief in terms of *de dicto* belief. Such theories seem to be inconsistent with the possibility of a certain type of *de re* explanation.

Heidelberger cites the following case:

Suppose there are two objects on a table, say a dish and a basket, and I am asked to remove the more valuable of the two and in response I remove the basket. To explain why I removed the basket and not the dish I might say: 'I believed of the basket, but not of the dish, that it was the more valuable'. Suppose further that I know that the basket and the dish are not equal in value—that one is more valuable than the other, and, contrary to my belief, the dish is the more valuable of the two. Since I know that the more valuable of the two objects is the more valuable of the two, on Chisholm's account of *de re* belief, I must believe of the dish, as well as of the basket, that it is the more valuable . . . [But if this were true, then] we would be unable to explain why I removed the basket and not the dish by saying, as I did above, that the former, but not the latter, is such that I believed it to be the more valuable.[7]

The explanation of the action, as Heidelberger says, should contain a statement saying what it is that the subject believed about the basket—and one having no analogue that is applicable to the dish. The general problem may be a serious one for any attempt—as my earlier theory was—to reduce *de re* belief to *de dicto* belief, but the problem is easy to deal with on the present account.

Of the two senses of *de re* belief that we have distinguished, the one that is applicable in the present case is the more rigid one: 'There exists a y such that a identifies y as a thing he believes to be F'. The subject of the above example perceives the basket and takes it to *be*, not only the basket, but also (so he thinks) the more valuable of the two objects, the basket and the dish. The statement needed in the explanation for the subject's action is this: 'The basket that is on his table is such that he identifies it as a thing which he believes to be, not only the basket, but also the more valuable of the two objects that are on his table'.

De Re Belief with Multiple Objects

We have considered cases of *de re* belief which are directed upon single objects ('x indirectly attributes to y the property of being F'). But *de re* beliefs may also be directed upon a number of objects. Thus I may believe, with respect to two things, x and y, that x is larger than y. How are we to deal with such cases?

Consider, for example, the general statement 'There exists an x, a y, and a z such that x believes y to be taller than z'. This type of statement presents a challenge to any theory of *de re* belief.

If we say that y is the object of x's belief, then we would have to say that 'taller than z' expresses the content of his belief. But if 'taller than z' expresses a content, then it must have a singular or referential property as its sense. And we have expressed a scepticism with respect to the existence of such properties. We have also said that no predicative expression containing free variables has a property as its sense.

We encounter analogous difficulties, of course, if we say that z is the object of x's belief and that 'smaller than y' expresses its content.

What other possible objects are there for the belief in question? One might say that the class or set of the two things, y and z, is the object. But what does one believe about that class or set—other than that one of its members, y, is taller than the other of its members, z?

There is also the ordered pair, x, y—i.e., that class having as its only members the class which has x as its only member and the class which has x and y as its only members. But how does one make *that* thing one's object? And what is it that one attributes to the ordered pair when one believes that y is taller than z? One answer to the latter question would be: 'being taller than'. But in such a situation can one readily say: 'There is something that x believes to be taller than'?

The problem can be dealt with very simply on the present account of *de re* belief. The statement 'There exists an x, a y, and a z such that x believes y to be taller than z' tells us this: 'There exists an x, a y, a z, a relation $R1$, and a relation $R2$ such that: x bears $R1$ to y and only to y; x bears $R2$ to z and only to z; and x directly attributes to himself a property which entails being such that, for every w, w has it if and only if the thing to which w bears $R1$ is taller than the thing to which w bears $R2$.'

Let us now consider a more complicated case. How might we paraphrase 'he and she both believe that I am taller than you' without appeal to singular propositions or to singular properties (e.g., that property, if there is one, which would be the sense of the expression 'being taller than you')? I would propose this:

There are relations $R1$, $R2$, $R3$ and $R4$ such that: (i) you are the thing to which he bears $R1$; (ii) you are the thing to which she bears $R2$; (iii) I am the thing to which he bears $R3$; (iv) I am the thing to which she bears $R4$; (v) he directly attributes to himself a property which is necessarily such that, for every x, x has that property if and only if the thing to which x bears $R3$ is taller than the thing to which x bears $R1$; and (vi) she directly attributes to herself a property which is necessarily such that, for every x, x has that property if and only if the thing to which x bears $R4$ is taller than the thing to which x bears $R2$.

What if I say to you: 'I believe that either Jones is ill or Smith is away'? What is the object of my belief in such a case? Even if there is that entity which is the *disjunctivum*, Jones or Smith, I am not saying with respect to *it* that either it is ill or it is away. And, of course, to believe that either Jones is ill or Smith is away is not the same as to be such that either one believes with respect to Jones that he is ill or that one believes with respect to Smith that he is away. What are we to say, then, of the object of such a belief?

My statement, 'I believe that Jones is ill or Smith is away', expresses my direct attribution to myself of a property of the following sort: there is a relation $R1$ which I bear to Jones and only to Jones; there is a relation $R2$ which I bear to Smith and only to Smith; and H is necessarily such that whatever has it bears $R1$ to just one thing and to a thing that is ill or bears $R2$ to just one thing and to a thing that is away. The *content* I want you to accept when I make such a statement need not include these relations, and in using the proper names 'Jones' and 'Smith', I assume that they will enable you to single out Jones and Smith. Since I am merely attributing such a property H to myself, there is no reason to suppose that the situation in question involves a complex propositional object.

Other problems for ontology are suggested by the following formula: 'J believes, with respect to K, that he, K, once thought that he, J, was F'.[8] If what we have been saying is correct, then this type of formula can be explicated as follows: 'There are relations, $R1$ and $R2$, and properties, F and G, such that: (i) J directly attributes H to J; (ii) H is necessarily such that, for every z, z has H, if and only if, z bears $R1$ to just one thing and to a thing which, when it has G, bore $R2$ to z and only to z; and (III) G is necessarily such that, for every y, y has G, if and only if, y bears $R2$ to just one thing and to a thing that is F'.

The following, somewhat more complex, formulae could be handled in an analogous way: 'John believes, with respect to Karl, that when he, John, was going to visit Boston, Karl thought that he, John, was planning to visit him'; and 'John believes, with respect to Karl, that he, Karl, once thought that when he, John, was going to visit Boston, he, John, was planning to meet him'.

It would be instructive to compare the ways in which other theories of reference and intentionality deal with such statements.

Conclusion

I have said that this book is, in part, a defence of certain ontological theses. These include the thesis that every property is 'pure' or 'qualitative'—no property is dependent for its existence upon anything that might not have existed. A corollary is the thesis that there are no singular or referential properties—no properties that require for their description a reference to some specific individual thing. If this latter thesis is true, then, as I have said, such expressions as 'being identical with John' and 'being the brother of Tom' do not have properties as their senses. I have also held that there are no 'singular propositions'—and hence that sentences containing demonstratives do not normally express propositions.

How does one support such a negative view—a view to the effect that there are no entities of a certain sort? First, one presupposes that entities are not to be multiplied beyond necessity. And then, secondly, one tries to show that such *grounds* or *reasons* as might be adduced for saying that there *are* such entities are inadequate.

The principal reason for supposing that there are such entities is the assumption that the analysis of objective reference and intentionality requires them, but we are now in a position to say that this assumption is false.

In this way, then, we defend the thesis of the primacy of the intentional.

Notes

1   Compare Ernest Sosa, 'Propositional Attitudes *De Dicto* and *De Re*', *Journal of Philosophy*, Vol. LXVII (1970), pp. 883–96.
2   Quine distinguishes 'There exists an x such that Witold wishes that x is President' and 'Witold wishes that there exists an x such that x is President'. He says that, according to the first, witold 'has his candidate' and that, according to the second, he 'merely wishes the appropriate form of government were in force'. W. V. Quine, *The Ways of Paradox* (New York: Random House, 1966), p. 185.
3   Strictly speaking, this definition of knowing is not adequate to what has come to be known as 'the Gettier problem' or 'the problem of the fourth condition'—a problem that is not relevant to our present concerns. The simplest way of dealing with that problem, I believe, is to replace 'it is evident' in the final clause of the definiens by: 'Either it is certain for x that he is F, or the property of being F is entailed by a conjunction of properties, each having for x a basis which is not a basis of any false attribution for x'. We could say that a self-presenting property is the *basis* for an attribution provided (a) that the subject has that property and (b) that necessarily, for anyone who has the property and for whom the attribution is epistemically in the clear, the attribution is evident. See

Edmund L. Gettier, 'Is Justified True Belief Knowledge?' *Analysis*, 22 (1963), pp. 121–3. Compare the second edition of my book *Theory of Knowledge*, Chapter 6; and Keith Lehrer, *Knowledge* (Oxford: The Clarendon Press, 1974), Chapter 9.
4 And what of 'makes evident'? If e makes h evident for S, then: e is evident for S; h is epistemically in the clear for S; and necessarily h is evident for anyone for whom e is evidence and h is epistemically in the clear.
5 David Kaplan, 'Quantifying In', *Synthese*, XIX (1968–69), pp. 178–214; see pp. 194–5.
6 Diana Ackerman, '*De Re* Propositional Attitudes toward Integers', *The Southwestern Journal of Philosophy*, IX (1979), pp. 145–53; see p. 150.
7 Herbert Heidelberger, 'The Self-Presenting', *Grazer Philosophische Studien* Vol. VII (1973). The general difficulty was first pointed out by Richard Feldman, 'Actions and *De Re* Beliefs', in *Canadian Journal of Philosophy*, Vol. VIII (1978), pp. 577–82.
8 Compare Castaneda's example: Privatus says: 'Once it occurred to Jones that I buried a letter here'. See 'Indicators and Quasi-Indicators', *American Philosophical Quarterly*, IV (1967), pp. 85–100.

Appendix
THE ONTOLOGY OF STATES OF AFFAIRS

Introduction

I CONSIDER here certain further details of the general ontology set forth in Chapter 2. I had discussed the relations between states of affairs and maintained: (i) that states of affairs may be divided into those that are compound and those that are non-compound; (ii) that non-compound states of affairs may be divided into those that are affirmative and those that are negative; and (iii) that *times*, as well as *possible worlds*, may be construed as being sub-species of states of affairs. I shall now defend these assertions.

This development of the theory does not require that we go beyond the primitive philosophical vocabulary already introduced, but it does require that we take *tense* seriously and that we introduce tensed forms of the 'is' of predication.

We make use, then, of six undefined philosophical concepts: that of *conceiving*, that of *obtaining*, that of *exemplifying*, that of a *relation*, that of *de re* possibility, and that of direct attribution.

The Structure of States of Affairs

I will now show how it is possible to distinguish states of affairs by reference to their structure. Without confusing states of affairs with the sentences that may be used to express them, we may distinguish among states of affairs those which are *conjunctions*, those which are *disjunctions*, and those which are *negations*. Any such state of affairs may be said to be *compound*. Then we will note the sense in which it is possible to divide non-compound states of affairs into those which are *affirmative* and those which are *negative*.

In Chapter 4, we defined *de dicto* belief—the *acceptance* of a state of affairs—in terms of direct attribution. We now use this concept of *acceptance* and that of *conceiving*—both of them intentional concepts—to exhibit the *structure* of states of affairs. Let us first introduce two relational concepts:

> D1 The state of affairs p involves the state of affairs q = Df. p is necessarily such that, whoever conceives it, conceives q.

> D2 The state of affairs p entails the state of affairs q = Df. p is necessarily such that (i) if it obtains then q obtains and (ii) whoever accepts it accepts q.

The state of affairs expressed by 'There being Greeks' *logically implies* that expressed by 'Either there being Greeks or there being Romans' (for the first is necessarily such that if it obtains then the second obtains). But the first does not *involve* the second (you can conceive the first without conceiving the second) and the first does not *entail* the second (you can accept the first without accepting the second). The state of affairs expressed by 'Either there being Greeks or there being Romans' *involves* that expressed by 'There being Romans', but it does not logically imply it or entail it. And the state of affairs expressed by 'There being Greeks and there being Romans' logically implies, involves and entails that expressed by 'There being Romans'.

Mutual involvement and mutual entailment provide us with intentional criteria of identity for states of affairs.

Now we are able to characterize *conjunctions*, *negations* and *disjunctions* of states of affairs.

> D3 c is a conjunction of p and q = Df. c is a state of affairs having the following property H; it entails p and entails q, and is such that everything it entails entails something that either p entails or q entails; and each thing having H entails c.

It may be observed that this definition of a *conjunction* of states of affairs is similar to Stanislaw Lesniewski's definition of *sum*.[1]

We next introduce a concept which is essential for characterizing the *negation* of a state of affairs, and which enables us to characterize non-compound states of affairs as being either positive or negative. This is the concept of *explicit contradiction*:

THE ONTOLOGY OF STATES OF AFFAIRS

D4 p explicitly denies q = Df. p is necessarily such that: it obtains if and only if q does not obtain; for every r, q involves r, if and only if, p involves r and r does not involve p.

(The final clause could also be put by saying: 'p properly involves just what q involves'. A state of affairs p 'properly involves' a state of affairs q, provided only that p involves q and q does not involve p.) This concept of explicit denial provides us with a mark of what we may call a *negative* state of affairs: a negative state of affairs is one that explicitly denies something. And so we may reject Frege's observation that 'it is by no means easy to state what is a negative judgment (thought)'.[2]

Each state of affairs and its negation are so related that one is negative and the other is not negative. We may now define the *negation* of a state of affairs:

D7 p is a negation of q = Df. Either p explicitly denies q, or q explicitly denies p.

Having a definition of negation, we may go on to define *disjunction* in a familiar way. A state of affairs d is a disjunction of states of affair p and q, provided only d is a negation of a conjunction of a negation of p and a negation of q.

A *compound* state of affairs, we have said, is one which is a conjunction, a disjunction or a negation. All other states of affairs are *non-compound*.[3]

Propositions and States of Affairs

There are philosophical arguments that are designed to show that 'tense is illusory' or 'time is unreal'. I would presume to say, however, that these arguments, once they are clearly formulated, are very easy to refute, and therefore that they are not worthy of our present consideration. I shall assume, then, that tense is to be taken seriously.

This assumption is reflected by the following principle about properties and states of affairs:

P1 For every property G, there are three states of affairs, p, q and r, which are necessarily such that: (i) p obtains if and only if *there exists* an x such that x has G; (ii) g obtains if and only if *there existed* an x such that x *did* have G; and (iii) r obtains if and only if *there will exist* an x such that x *will have G*.

An analogous principle holds for relations (but such a principle will be more complex inasmuch as things that do not coexist may yet be related to each other.)

I have used temporal quantifiers ('there does exist', 'there did exist' and 'there will exist') in the formulation of the above principle. But, given tense, temporal relations and the fact that there are eternal objects, we need only the present-tense quantifier. For 'there *existed* an x such that x was F' can be construed as telling us that there *exists* a y which *did have* the property of being such that there *exists* such that x is F. And 'there will exist an x such that x will be F' tells us that there exists a y which will have the property of being such that there exists an x such that x is F. In each case, any eternal object will satisfy the description of y. (An alternative method of eliminating past-tensed and future-tensed quantifiers will be set forth below.)

Up to now, we have used 'state of affairs' and 'proposition' more or less interchangeably, but we may now single out *propositions* as being those states of affairs which are necessarily such that they are invariable in their truth-value.

D6 p is a proposition = Df. p is a state of affairs which is necessarily such that either it obtains at all times or it obtains at no time.

We may say that a proposition is *true* if and only if it obtains, and otherwise that it is *false*.

Our definition, however, contains the term 'times'.

Times

It is now possible to explicate *times*, not as being an irreducible type of entity, but as being a certain type of *state of affairs*.

Suppose we wanted to describe the present state of the world, but without giving any hints or clues about the way things have been or the way they are going to be. We could do this if we restricted ourselves to what might be called *strict attributes*—

attributes which imply nothing about the past or the future of the things that have them. (More exactly, a *strict attribute* would be a non-universal property such that it is possible for a thing to have it without having previously existed and it is possible for a thing to have it without subsequently existing.) Walking is a strict attribute, since it is possible—logically possible—for a thing to have the property of walking without having the property of being such that it did walk, and it is possible for a thing to have the property of walking without having the property of being such that it will walk. (But I would say that it is necessarily the case that whatever is walking is such that *either* it did walk *or* it will walk.) By restricting ourselves to such attributes, then, we could describe the world in a way that would restrict us to the present moment. Of course, we wouldn't be able to say how *old* different things are, or how much time they had left. But if I report how old you are or how much time you have left, I *am* giving some clue concerning the nature of the past or the future.

Let us introduce the following concept:

D7 p is a world-state = Df. p is a state of affairs which possibly obtains; and for every strict attribute a, either p is necessarily such that if it obtains then something has A or p is necessarily such that if it obtains then nothing has A.

A world-state, then, will be neither necessary nor impossible.

Now we may consider defining *times* in terms of 'minimal' world-states.

D8 p is a time = Df. p is a world-state which is implied by every world-state it implies.

Let us note that 'there is a time t such that . . .' will become 'there is a world-state t such that . . .' and we may say 'there *is*', even for past and future times, since states of affairs are eternal objects. Thus: to say 'p obtains at time t' is to say that the conjunction, p and t, obtains; to say 'p obtained at t' is to say that the conjunction, p and t, did obtain; and to say 'p will obtain at t' is to say that the conjunction, p and t, will obtain.

We now have an alternative way of reducing the past-tensed and future-tensed quantifiers to the present-tense quantifier.

Thus 'there existed an x such that x was F' becomes 'there exists a time t such that the conjunction of t and *there being an x such that x is F* did obtain'. And 'there will exist an x such that x will be F' becomes 'there exists a time t such that the conjunction of t and *there being an x such that x is F* will obtain'.

The relations *earlier* and *later* may be characterized in a similar way. For example, the past-tensed 'p obtained later than g did' would be 'p was such that: it obtains, q does not obtain, and q did obtain'.

If times are states of affairs, then, strictly speaking, there will *be* times that do not *obtain*. The ordinary philosophical use of the expression 'There is a time such that . . .' may be explicated as "Either there obtains or did obtain or will obtain a time such that . . .'"

Our definitions have the consequence that it is logically possible for a time to occur more than once. There *is* therefore a sense in which we can say that it is possible for the past to be brought back.

Could it be brought back with the original cast? Even that is possible—provided the original cast has survived. If the same world-state were to occur twice, we could 'individuate' the two occurrences by reference to the ages of the actors. But how are we to specify the ages of the actors?

Let us consider those states of affairs that may be said to be 'mere reflections of the past' or 'mere reflections of the future'. We could say: 'G is a mere reflector of a previous H', provided only: G is necessarily such that whatever has it had H; and G implies not strict attribute. And we could say: 'G is a mere reflector of a subsequent H', provided only: G is necessarily such that whatever has it will have H; and G implies no strict attribute.

My past reflectors, then, will include such properties as having been an infant and having been a boy. The future reflectors are, epistemically, more problematic. It should be noted that growing older is a matter of adding to one's past reflectors and subtracting from one's future reflectors.

It is, however, important to note that, from the fact that a given world-state recurs, it does not follow that *other* world-states recur. Hence we need not accept Prior's conclusion: '. . . if we have had it all at least n times before we have had it all at least $n + 1$ times before; so that if we have had it all once before there is no limit to the number of times we have had it all before.'[4]

Worlds

I shall now introduce a conception of 'possible worlds' which, I believe, is essentially that of Liebniz and other philosophers in the Western tradition, but it is unlike that presupposed by most contemporary philosophers. It does not go beyond the ontology involved in assuming that there are individuals, properties and relations, and states of affairs. It does not require us to assume that there *are* things which are 'merely possible entities'. Moreover, it does not require us to say that, if I have unrealized possibilities, then I exist 'in' other possible worlds. And it does not presuppose that individual things have individual essences or haecceities.

Let us introduce the concept of 'a world':

D9 W is a world = Df. W is a state of affairs; for every state of affairs p, either W logically implies p or W logically implies the negation of p; and there is no state of affairs q such that W logically implies both q and the negation of q.

It will be noted that I have defined 'a *world*', not 'a *possible world*'. I have avoided 'possible world', since the expression 'There are possible worlds' may suggest that there *are* certain things—worlds—somehow lying between being and non-being. But traditionally, when philosophers have spoken of 'possible worlds', I believe that, in so far as they can be understood, the concept they have had in mind can be explicated by reference to those states of affairs that are here called 'worlds'. If this is so and if states of affairs are eternal objects existing whether or not they obtain, then *all* so-called 'possible worlds' exist. Hence I use 'world' and not 'possible world'.

'But you can't mean to say that all possible worlds are *actual* worlds. There is—and can be—only *one* actual world!' The word 'actual' is here ambiguous. If 'x is actual' is taken to mean the same as 'x exists', then all possible worlds are actual. But when it is said that only one world is actual, then 'is actual' is taken to mean the same as 'obtains'. There is—and can be—only one world that *obtains*.

Hence we should avoid the temptation to speak of 'the real world' or 'the actual world'. Let us, rather, speak of 'the *world that obtains*', or 'the *prevailing world*'.

If a world is a state of affairs, and if states of affairs are eternal objects, what could it mean to say of an individual thing that it exists 'in a world'? How could you or I exist 'in a state of affairs'? We may *give* a meaning to this use of 'in':

D10 x exists in W = Df. W is a world; and either (a) x has an essence H such that W implies H or (b) W obtains and x exists.

(The *essence* of a thing x, we have said, is a property which is such that x necessarily has it and nothing else can possibly have it.) Our definition does not presuppose that individual things have individual essences, nor does it presuppose that they do not. It allows us to say that I exist in the prevailing world ('the actual world') even if I have no individual essence, but it does not allow us to say that I exist in any *other* world unless I have an individual essence that is implied by that world.

Even if I do not have an individual essence, *some* of my properties are essential to me—i.e., some of my properties are such that I have them necessarily. Suppose that *being a person* is such a property. Now there are some worlds which do not entail the property of being a person ('Some possible worlds don't contain any persons'). If I am necessarily a person, then I am necessarily such that none of those impersonal worlds obtains. Hence we may say that I *exclude* such worlds. (Or, if one prefers, one could put it the other way round and say that I am such that I am excluded by certain worlds.) We may say that a thing x *excludes* a world W, provided only x is necessarily such that W does not obtain. It should be noted that, from the fact that I am *not* excluded by a certain world W, it does not follow that I *exist in* in that world W.

But if I am not excluded by W, then I am *eligible* for W: that is to say, I am possibly such that W obtains.

If I were to have an essence E such that there is a certain world W that implies E (i.e., a certain world W which is necessarily such that if it obtains then something exemplifies E), then we could say that W is necessarily such that I exist. But if I have no individual essence, then we cannot say of *any* world that it is necessarily such that I exist. And we cannot even say this of 'the actual world'—i.e., the world that obtains. The latter point may be put somewhat loosely by saying that this world could have obtained without me. If the world had obtained without me, then someone else would have played my role. Indeed, if neither you nor I have individual essences, then the prevailing world could have obtained with you playing my role and me playing yours. One might say, paradoxically, that you and I would have been very different but the world would have been the same; this gives us a use for the label 'existentialism'.

Suppose a thing has a certain property necessarily. What does this imply with respect to those characteristics that the prevailing world has necessarily? Next to nothing, I would say. For example, Socrates may be necessarily such that he is a person. It does not follow from this either (a) that Socrates is necessarily such that he is a *person in this world*, or (b) that this world is necessarily such that if Socrates exists then he is a person.

The fact that I exist only in the prevailing world—if it is a fact—does not restrict my possibilities. The unrealized possibilities of a given individual are not to be explicated in terms of the different worlds in which that individual might be said to exist. We may speak of such possibilities, using the undefined *de re* modal locution with which we began: 'x is possibly such that it is F'. And so we may say, of a person who is not a lawyer, 'He could be a lawyer'. This does not tell us that he is a lawyer 'in some possible world'. It tells us no more nor less than that he is possibly such that he is a lawyer.

'But doesn't "He is possibly such that he is a lawyer" imply that he has an individual essence that is compatible with his being a lawyer?' No; the statement 'He is possibly such that he is a lawyer' does *not* mean that he has a nature that is compatible with being a lawyer. It means, rather, that he does *not* have a nature that is *incompatible* with his being a lawyer.

'If he is possibly such that he is a lawyer, and if he's not a lawyer in the prevailing world, then isn't it the case that, if he *were* a lawyer, he would be a lawyer *in another world*?' This is correct. But from this fact it does not follow that he *is* a lawyer in any other world. For, unless he has an individual essence, any other world could obtain without him.

Notes

1 See Alfred Tarski, *Logic, Semantics, Metamathematics* (Oxford: The Clarendon Press, 1956), p. 249.
2 From Frege's 'Negation', in P. Greach and M. Black, eds., *Translations from*

the Philosophical Writings of Gottlob Frege (Oxford: B. Blackwell, 1952), p. 125. Frege goes on to say: 'Consider the sentences "Christ is immortal", "Christ is mortal", "Christ does not live forever". Now which of the thoughts we have here is affirmative, which negative?' The answer is that they are all affirmative, provided that the 'is not' in the third example is read as 'is such that he is not', and that the 'does not' of the fifth example is read as 'is such that he does not'. But 'It is false that Christ is immortal' and 'It is false that Christ lives forever' would be negative.
3 In working out these definitions, I have been helped by criticisms from Herbert Heidelberger, Walter Horn, Erich Kraemer and Peter Tovey.
4 Arthur Prior, *Past, Present and Future* (Oxford: The Clarendon Press, 1967), p. 84.

INDEX

abstract objects, 4, 11, 45–6
acceptability, epistemic, 77–8, 99–100
acceptance, propositional, 38–40, 123–4
Ackerman, D., 73, 116–17, 122
access, privileged, 22, 43–5
Alston, W., 91
Anscombe, E., vii, 18, 21, 26, 35, 44, 45–6, 87, 91
appearing, 79–81, 93–5, 96, 102–3
apperception, 105
   transcendental unity of, 88
a priori, 39, 83–5
attribute, strict, 26–7
attribution, direct, 1, 27–8, 61, 75, 86
attribution, indirect, 29–40, 58–9, 70–1, 103, 107, 109–10, 115–16
axioms, 83–5

Baker, L., 73
belief: see attribution
'believes that' principle, 64–5, 67
Black, M., 131
Brentano, F., 16, 26, 87–8, 91, 104, 106
Butler, J., 78, 91
Burks, A., 53, 73

Carnap, R., 12
Cartwright, R., 73
Castaneda, H. N., 18, 22, 26, 35, 53, 122
Carneades, 99
certainty, 23, 75–91
classes, 8–9
conceiving, 7, 9, 37, 39, 123–5
confirmation, 99, 101
considering, 28, 29, 39–40, 80–1, 114–15
content of attribution, 1, 28, 29, 30, 35–7, 44, 56, 61, 75, 120
contradiction, explicit, 98–9, 124–5

Davidson, D., 73

Descartes, R., 80, 91
demonstratives, 8, 35–6, 39, 41–53
   temporal, 49–53
denominatio mere extrinsica, 13
de dicto attitudes, 14, 19, 64
de re attitudes, 13, 15, 19, 31, 66, 107–21
de re epistemic locution, 102–3
descriptions, definite, 71–2
description, under a, 33–5, 113
descriptive functions, 30
designators, rigid, 71–3
designatum, 45, 62
disjunctivum, 119
Donnellan, K., 40, 73
Dretske, F., 106

emphatic reflexive, 17–29, 34–5, 44
entailment, 7, 33
entertaining: see considering
epistemic concepts, 76–9
epistemically unsuspect, the, 97–100, 101
epistemology, 92
essences, 11, 37–8, 54, 75, 130–1
eternal objects: see abstract objects
events, 11
evidence
   perceptual, 101–3
   presumptive, 100–1
   transcendent, 72–102
evident, the, 78–9
   directly, 83, 84
exclusion, 10
exemplification, 4, 5
expression, 42, 61–2
existentialism, 131

Feigl, H., 73
Feldman, R., 122
first person pronoun, 2, 16, 42–9, 85–6

first person propositions, 1, 2, 15ff., 41ff., 75
first person sentences, 2, 15ff., 41ff.
Frege, G., 3, 16, 26, 72, 74, 125, 131–2

Geach, P., 18, 26, 131
Gettier, E., 121–2

haecceity: see essence
Haller, R., vii
Harmon, G., 73
hearer's meaning, 47, 60, 61, 62, 69–70
Heidelberger, H., vii, 117–18, 122, 123
Henrich, D., 26, 91
'here', 48
hermeneutics, 106
Horn, W., 132
Husserl, E., 16, 26, 47, 52

identifying property, 11, 15, 22, 45, 109–13
intentionality, the primacy of, 1, 42, 121
intimacy, epistemic, 109–13
involvement, 124–5

justification, epistemic, 2

Kamp, H., 53
Kant, I., 85, 88–9, 91
Kaplan, D., 46, 52, 73, 115–16, 122
Kasher, A., vii
Katkov, G., vii
knowing, 110
Kraemer, E., 132
Kripke, S., 66, 71, 73
Kung, G., 91

Lehrer, K., 73, 122
Leibniz, G. W., 105, 129
Lewis, D., 3, 32, 40
Lewis, H. D., vii
Lesniewski, S., 124
Locke, J., 96

Mach, E., 18, 26
Margalit, A., 73
Marty, A., 65, 73
Meinong, A., 100, 101, 106

memory, 105
mistaken indication, 69–70

negative existentials, 67–9
Neurath, O., 97, 106
negative existentials, 67–9
'now', 49–53
numbers, 9

obtaining, 9, 51, 126–30
object of attribution, 2, 29, 35–7
  multiple, 70–1, 118–20, 41, 44, 55–7
  primary, 32
ontology, 4, 123–32
opposition, positive, 104

perception, 95–7, 101–6, 109–10
  negative, 104–5
Perry, J., 3, 26
places, 48
Plantinga, A., 55, 73
Platonism, iv
Pollock, J., 106
possibility, 9–10, 131
possible worlds, 4, 71, 129–32
predicative expressions, 8
Price, H. H., 29, 40, 100–1, 106
Prior, A. N., 128, 132
primary uses, 41–3, 45
proper names, 39, 54–73
proper name fallacy, 54–6, 67
properties, 5–9, 40
  Cartesian, 79, 80
  identifying, 14–17, 45, 55, 58–9, 68
  indexical, 8, 46, 55
  normative, 82–3
  sensible, 96
propositions, 38–40, 54–6, 125–6
  necessary, 39
  singular, 4, 11, 22
  see: first person propositions, states of affairs
psychological, 25

Quine, W. V., 31, 58, 62, 108, 121

reference of words, 41, 45, 61–3
relations, 6, 9
  identifying, 29–33, 60
  intentional, 38

Renear, A., 40
Richter, Jean Paul, 90, 91
Russell, B., 8, 12, 30, 45, 49, 52, 104, 106

Searles, J., 73
sense, 41, 45, 46, 54–7, 117
   attributive, 57–8
   demonstrative, 58–9, 61–2
   secondary, 58, 60, 61, 62–3, 65–6
self, 86–91
self-presenting, the, 79–83, 94, 96–7
Sellars, W., 73
sets, 8–9
Sextus Empiricus, 106
Sleigh, R., 53
scepticism, 13–14
Sosa, E., vii, 106, 108, 121
Spiegelberg, H., 91
speaker's meaning, 14, 47, 60, 61, 62, 69–70, 85–6
speech acts, 61–2
Spinoza, B., 7, 12
states of affairs, 9–12, 38–40, 123–32
   compound, 123–5
   conjunctive, 124–5
   disjunctive, 125
   negative, 124–5
   sum, 124
supervenience, 82
suppositio materialis, 65

Tarski, A., 131
temporal quantifiers, 126–8
tense, 49–52, 125
'then', 51–2
'this', 21, 45–7, 49–50, 73
time, 4, 49–53, 125–8
Tovey, P., 132

unity of consciousness, 85–91

Vesey, G., vii, 48

Whitehead, A. N., 12, 35–6, 40, 105, 106
withholding, 76
Wittgenstein, L., 1, 2, 3, 5, 32, 58, 67–8, 73–4
Wolterstorff, N., 53
worlds, 129–32
world-states, 127–8

'you', 48–9